Cambridge Elements ≡

Elements in Language, Gender and Sexuality
edited by
Helen Sauntson
York St John University
Holly R. Cashman
University of New Hampshire

QUEERING SEXUAL HEALTH TRANSLATION PEDAGOGY

Piero Toto
London Metropolitan University

CAMBRIDGE
UNIVERSITY PRESS

CAMBRIDGE
UNIVERSITY PRESS

Shaftesbury Road, Cambridge CB2 8EA, United Kingdom

One Liberty Plaza, 20th Floor, New York, NY 10006, USA

477 Williamstown Road, Port Melbourne, VIC 3207, Australia

314–321, 3rd Floor, Plot 3, Splendor Forum, Jasola District Centre,
New Delhi – 110025, India

103 Penang Road, #05–06/07, Visioncrest Commercial, Singapore 238467

Cambridge University Press is part of Cambridge University Press & Assessment,
a department of the University of Cambridge.

We share the University's mission to contribute to society through the pursuit of
education, learning and research at the highest international levels of excellence.

www.cambridge.org
Information on this title: www.cambridge.org/9781009467834

DOI: 10.1017/9781009221023

First published 2023

A catalogue record for this publication is available from the British Library

ISBN 978-1-009-46783-4 Hardback
ISBN 978-1-009-22098-9 Paperback
ISSN 2634-8772 (online)
ISSN 2634-8764 (print)

Cambridge University Press & Assessment has no responsibility for the persistence
or accuracy of URLs for external or third-party internet websites referred to in this
publication and does not guarantee that any content on such websites is, or will
remain, accurate or appropriate.

Queering Sexual Health Translation Pedagogy

Elements in Language, Gender and Sexuality

DOI: 10.1017/9781009221023
First published online: November 2023

Piero Toto
London Metropolitan University

Author for correspondence: Piero Toto, p.toto@londonmet.ac.uk

Abstract: Sexual health campaigns to tackle the rise in sexually transmitted infections in England are at the core of sexual health charities' and grassroots organizations' work. Some of them collaborated with the author's translation students to produce inclusive translations of their sexual health content (website and multimedia content). The role of translation and localization within multicultural contexts can be seen as 'social activism' promoting sexual health and community engagement, with a view to providing wider healthcare access and information using inclusive language. This Element presents students' approaches to sexual health translation, using language as a vessel for change and striking a balance between clients' expectations, translation industry best practices, and socio-educational needs. The data analysis of the students' experiences will make the case for wider embedding of queer pedagogy approaches into the translation curriculum.

This Element also has a video abstract: www.cambridge.org/Piero_Toto

Keywords: queer translation, sexual health, translation pedagogy, web localization, social activism

ISBNs: 9781009467834 (HB), 9781009220989 (PB), 9781009221023 (OC)
ISSNs: 2634-8772 (online), 2634-8764 (print)

Contents

1 The Context

Sexual health campaigns to tackle the rise in sexually transmitted infections in England are at the core of sexual health charities' and grassroots organizations' work. In multi-ethnic and multicultural societies such as the UK, it has become increasingly necessary for these campaigns to be made available in a variety of languages, and not just English, in order to cater for the needs of various communities as well as to address inequalities in access to sexual health information and care. Since these campaigns rely predominantly on online dissemination and high impact, it is important to be able to retain these features in their translated versions too. In the study that follows, a sexual health campaign originally integrating inclusive language was assigned to the author's undergraduate translation students as part of a simulated translation project management module. The students worked in groups mimicking the dynamics of a translation agency and, at the end, they were asked to reflect via a questionnaire on their experience of translating sexual health materials and having to deal with sex-related terminology. The discussion surrounding these topics was underpinned by queer pedagogy approaches and the contextualization of the practice of translation, as will be explained in the ensuing sections, which make the case for wider embedding of queer pedagogy approaches into the translation curriculum.

2 What Is Sexual Health?

Sexual health has become an increasingly used phrase and debated topic since the early 2000s. Defined by Richman Davidow (2018), amongst others, as encompassing a wide range of attributes, from identity and body image to sexually transmitted infections (STIs), to consent, gender, and sexual orientation, it is at the centre of prevention campaigns and education efforts. Although definitions of sexual health have changed since its original 1975 World Health Organization (WHO) definition and in the knowledge that human needs are becoming more and more holistic, the definition that will underpin this case study will be the current WHO working definition of sexual health, namely:

> a state of physical, emotional, mental, and social well-being in relation to sexuality; it is not merely the absence of disease, dysfunction or infirmity. Sexual health requires a positive and respectful approach to sexuality and sexual relationships, as well as the possibility of having pleasurable and safe sexual experiences, free of coercion, discrimination and violence. For sexual health to be attained and maintained, the sexual rights of all persons must be respected, protected and fulfilled. (WHO, 2006, p. 5)

A pre-Covid-19 report by Public Health England (2019) provides a snapshot of sexual health services and infections without being affected by the disruption that occurred as a result of the pandemic. It acknowledged a rise in STIs, notably chlamydia and syphilis, due to increased condomless sex activity; this rise has prompted the launch of more direct and impactful sexual health campaigns by sexual health charities and grassroots organizations on top of nationally directed programmes. Sometimes these campaigns may present issues in the way they address their intended audience, either by being too specific – and therefore excluding certain other members of the public – or by employing unintentionally biased language. In an effort to draw attention to the language used in these campaigns due to the bias that could be conveyed implicitly when talking about a disease or a condition, it has been suggested, for example, that when dealing with HIV, *people-first* language should be used (The Well Project, 2021), meaning that one should describe what a person *has* rather than what a person *is* and, therefore, 'person with HIV' should be used instead of 'HIV patient'. In this way, stigma is avoided in communication and effective education about diseases, infections, conditions, or groups of people can happen (The Well Project, 2021).

Sexual health is essential to the development of healthy and nurturing relationships that are the foundation of successful futures both personally and professionally. To ensure the importance of these aspects of sexual health in language communities (e.g. culturally diverse settings), it is necessary to translate sexual health materials using culturally responsive and culturally sensitive language that extends beyond the language of heterosexuality and the gender binary, thus preventing people's sexual needs from being diminished and their identities 'otherized'. The failure to recognize the importance of language in translating the sexual health needs of transgender and non-binary individuals, for example, has consistently impeded access to healthcare services and positive sexual health outcomes across all continents and has historically determined a costly gap in multicultural health promotion due to a lack of culturally effective, motivational, and multicultural health promotion resources (Ji et al., 2020). In the next section, the role of translation will be highlighted and outlined as a pedagogical instrument to convey socially relevant messages which contribute to students' co-creation of meanings in specific contexts.

3 Translation as an Interdiscipline for Change

Translation as both an academic discipline and a professional occupation can be defined as 'a set of practices and processes crucial to communication within and between cultures' (Malmkjær, 2022, p. 1) involving the transfer of a message from one language to another; it is 'a communicative event which is shaped by its own goals, pressures and context of production' (Baker, 1996, p. 175). The communicative element of translation is core to its nature and often results in a 'socially mediated and ideologically constructed practice' (Spurlin, 2014b, p. 202). *Socially mediated* means that it relies on an exchange, outward-facing contact consisting of interactions involving translators, project managers (PMs), clients and other agents, depending on the type of translation product involved. These stakeholders are expected to abide by certain standards of practice and codes of conduct which regulate these exchanges (ATC, 2019; CIOL, 2017; ITI, 2013) or at least to acknowledge and implement industry-recognized practices. *Ideologically constructed* means that 'translators use translation for ideological purposes that are overtly aligned with the organizations and political and cultural movements they represent' (Baker, 2010, p. 260). Translation can be seen as the ultimate form of intercultural transfer, making a source text available to readers and speakers of a different language and culture (Munday, 2007). As part of this transfer and as stated by Hatim and Mason (1997), the translator's activity may show ideological traits which may be imbued in the translations themselves regardless of genre (translation of ideology) or which may elicit an ideological interpretation on the part of the translator (ideology of translation). This can happen regardless of genre and text typology, hence affecting a wide spectrum of potential translation products, such as literary texts, political texts, news reports, medical documents, and websites. Ideology here will be understood as 'the voicing and stance of the translator' (Tymoczko, 2003, p. 183) whereby language expressions and linguistic devices are employed as tools through which ideology can be articulated both in the original text and in translation, including: the experiential representation of reality (e.g. the way one uses the passive voice, nominalizations, or patterns of transitivity); evaluation (i.e. the way one uses adverbs to convey or colour expressions); and overall textual coherence (i.e. whether a text holds up by itself and the links across its subunits) (Munday, 2007). Translation therefore cannot be divorced from ideology, which is frequently inscribed in language use; hence 'translation that engages in a transfer from one language into another language is selected as an effective tool of ideological operation' (Shih, 2010).

Through their translation acts, translators delicately balance degrees of interference (consciously or unconsciously) with the text and act as 'agent[s] of linguistic and cultural alienation' (Venuti, 2017, p. 307) in a constant tug of war between submission and resistance:

> Every step in the translation process – from the selection of foreign texts to
> the implementation of translation strategies to the editing, reviewing, and
> reading of translations – is mediated by the diverse cultural values that

> circulate in the target language, always in some hierarchical order. The
> translator, who works with varying degrees of calculation, under continuous
> self-monitoring and often with active consultation of cultural rules and
> resources (from dictionaries and grammars to other texts, translation strat-
> egies, and translations, both canonical and marginal), may submit to or resist
> dominant values in the target language, with either course of action suscep-
> tible to ongoing redirection. (Venuti, 2017, p. 308)

This constant tension in the exchanges and negotiation of interest between the
source system and the target system, where 'system' here includes both the
language and the culture, is at the heart of every translation-mediated transfer
requiring human agency (Bassnett, 2011; Carlson & Corliss, 2011), where
'shifts' occur brought about by ideology or mere style preferences (Munday,
2014). The aforementioned tension manifests itself in the application of the
translation act to queer sexuality, whereby translation can both erase or highlight the queer experience and its understanding to otherwise ill-informed
audiences (Baer, 2021). The role of the translator can therefore be regarded as
that of a gatekeeper, that is, a controller of the quantity and quality of information transferred during the translation process on the basis of the perceived or
effective needs of the target text receivers but also on the basis of the instruc-
tions that they may have received and/or, more generally, their own ideology.[1]
As such, translations can be recognized as an art form as well as a laborious
practice and, most importantly, as a tool used in combination with language 'for
legitimizing the *status quo* or for subverting it' (Castro, 2013a, p. 6, original
italics). This may introduce elements in the translation which may not have been
present in the source material.

As observed by Xie (2018, p. 80) in relation to the liminal space occupied by
translation:

> one of the most significant events that has happened in translation studies is
> the change of translation from its role as a passive, invisible, neutral trans-
> mitter of messages to its new role as an active, free, creative participant in the
> production of meaning ... Over the past few decades what has been most
> productively discussed of translation is its ethical and political agency in the
> age of globalization and the role it plays in vindicating and rehabilitating
> marginalized and mistreated ethnic/cultural Others; increasing awareness of
> cultural and lingual diversity . . ..

Because of the nature of their role, translators can be 'submissive to or subversive
of the original text and its author' (Lee, 2022, p. 6), whereby the translation
resulting out of this dynamic process can be defined as a performative act where

---

[1] As Castro (2013b) points out, depending on the translation workflow, this role may also be
adopted by proofreaders, copy-editors, editors, clients, patrons, publishers, and so on.

'translating [is seen] as "doing", doing something *to* the target reader' (Robinson, 2003, p. 16, original italics). It is therefore vital to acknowledge that using translation as a pedagogical tool to recognize the performative nature of the translation act, as well as its transformative and transgressive power, allows students to learn by doing, to feel empowered in their communication skills. The underlying and inherent dynamics at play in each culture and language may produce a situation whereby subverting the original is not an option and, as a matter of fact, the act of subversion affects the target language instead, so that 'what seems resistant in the space of English may be reactionary in the space of the original language' (Spivak, 1992/2012, p. 319).

Translation as a pedagogical tool has a long history of revitalizing sociocultural fields of knowledge (see, for example, Laviosa, 2014a, 2014b; Pym et al., 2013) and investigating interlingual modes of knowledge transfer and communication (e.g. audiovisual translation and language learning). As Floros (2020) states, in order for translation teaching to be effective in strengthening communicative competence, as is required in language teaching and learning today, it is necessary to introduce exercises that emphasize translation as a communicative activity, simulating the communicative conditions, including the relevant technologies, that students find in real life. Effective pedagogy involves understanding the needs and interests of learners, creating a positive and engaging learning environment, using appropriate teaching methods and materials, and providing feedback and assessment to support learners' progress. Pedagogy also involves critical reflection and ongoing evaluation of teaching practices to ensure that they are effective and responsive to the changing needs of learners and society. It is specifically this latter aspect which will be examined in the case study proposed here. The pedagogy of translation, however, has its challenges too, which are mostly aligned with the challenges of pedagogy as practice, namely keeping students engaged and motivated to learn, balancing the demands of curriculum requirements with the need for creativity and innovation in teaching and adapting to changing educational practices, amongst others (Markey et al., 2023). The need to introduce and foreground exercises focusing on communicative activities is paramount to framing translation as a pedagogically transformative discipline and act: the impact that a finished and published translated product can have on the relevant target communities and consumers can be life-changing, as is often the case with sexual health campaigns that directly impact (and save) people's lives. For students to realize and fully acknowledge their role in this process is greatly empowering and it prepares them for the challenges ahead in the translation industry, be it on the commercial or the editorial/literary side of things, as well as confronting them with ethical and moral issues with which they would otherwise not be faced.

In an effort to break away from the heteronormative implications of language, applying a queer perspective and queer practices to the act of translation, therefore, seeks to reclaim power through changing the way we conceptualize language itself. Within translation studies, the concept of queering translation has recently come to the forefront of the discipline. It stems from the reappropriation of the slur 'queer' – originally identifying gays and lesbians – which 'refers to that which is not aligned with any particular identity and resists categorisations' (Sauntson, 2008, p. 272). It refers to its application to a field of knowledge which has been historically open to methodological experimentations (Zanettin & Rundle, 2022). Building on gender studies and feminist studies, queer translation here will be intended as translating sexuality, or the sexualization of translation, which involves the application of strategies aimed at inclusivity, transparency and an appreciation of the complexities/nuances of queer identity and culture.

Because of the need to disassociate biomedical knowledge from prevailing heteronormative ideas of sexual health and rights, new queer approaches to public health have been adopted (Spurlin, 2019), in particular a shift in the way sexual health agencies translate their information in order to better serve the LGBTQ+ communities. By queering perspectives on health and sexual education, it is possible to learn how to make healthcare more inclusive and what changes need to be made to reach this goal. When used in combination with translation, it allows the latter to fully realize its potential as a pedagogical tool and to foreground the translator as

> an ideological mediator who has to negotiate a double ethical responsibility. One is their responsibility towards the source (con)text, to convey the content of a previous text in the most thorough and convenient possible way. The other, their responsibility towards the target (con)text, which includes paying attention to the cultural and linguistic changes in vogue in the target society so as to be able to produce an 'updated' translation in accordance with them – without preventing the target audience from getting to know how the source text was addressing its source audience. (Castro, 2013b, p. 40)

The translation of queer sexual health information is therefore a feminist act (Kincheloe, 2008): it concedes that knowledge is inherently relational and social, not just in terms of how we learn new things, but also how we define them. In order to respect audiences, their needs must be honoured; students must become aware of what they are doing and tutors must allow themselves to learn alongside their students, rather than expecting everyone to be at the same starting level. Non-LGBTQ+ students may never have had these conversations with friends or family members and can feel left out of conversations that are pertinent to their lives and future. Educators have an obligation to prepare students for a world in which they will encounter people who think differently from them on all kinds of issues, including gender, race, sexuality, and social class. Tutors must be prepared to provide their students with opportunities to reflect on their own biases as well as those of others. This exchange of knowledge through difference is at the heart of queer practices of learning which imply some level of negotiation of meanings (Luhmann, 1998).

Queer pedagogy, which will be further explored in Section 4, offers students a safe space to learn and to be open to what they have to say. Queering sexual health translation involves the employment of queer theoretical and methodological perspectives in rendering materials available in a variety of languages, bearing in mind their potential reach beyond the geographical borders in which they are originally conceived. This implies a conscious effort and attention to nuances and an acknowledgement of difference (Britzman, 1995), as well as between cultures and people speaking the same language but belonging to different countries or being located in the same country of production of the original sexual health material. This ties in well with translation as a discipline whose meanings are expressed both at the textual and the cultural/transcultural level (Spurlin, 2014a).

Queer sexual health recognizes all forms of sexuality, including non-binary and non-traditional expressions of sexuality, identity, and body. Translating this into public health efforts, such as sex education and sexual health promotion, means embracing an inclusive definition of sexual health and providing information that supports the health needs of all people, regardless of their gender or sexual identities. As explained by Carcelén-Estrada (2018, p. 254), 'translation as a poetic, political act plays the ambiguous role of creating borders between native and foreign languages and peoples while opening spaces for alternative modes of thinking that seek to redraw and even erase these same borders'. Accepting or promoting dominant ideologies or systemic practices, without questioning their truth value, may harm marginalized communities, such as transgender or non-heterosexual individuals; by querying such information instead, there exists a chance to critically alter the way people think about things like sex, sexual orientation, or even just health education models in general. New theories are also introduced that may be more helpful than those offered through traditional gendered epistemologies when dealing with issues involving sexual education, thus empowering alternative forms of knowledge that may help people who traditionally suffer under normative ways of thinking. These new understandings can then be spread within certain communities, depending on who should receive that information. As a pedagogical tool, therefore, translation acts as a catalyst for the promotion of intercultural communication. An effective pedagogy of translation involves providing learners with clear objectives, appropriate materials, and constructive feedback, as well as encouraging resourcefulness and reliance on prior learning and knowledge, in order to inform their practice and to help them develop a well-rounded set of skills (linguistic or otherwise). The integration of queer-centred discourses into translation activities is a way of creating a more inclusive and welcoming learning environment for all students, and of fostering respect and empathy for diverse perspectives and experiences. The next section will provide an overview of queer pedagogy as an instrument for social justice and will frame it as an 'added-value tool' within the interdisciplinary nature of translation.

4 Queer Pedagogy and Translation

Queer pedagogy is an approach to teaching and learning that challenges hetero-normative assumptions and addresses issues of social justice and inclusivity for people who identify as lesbian, gay, bisexual, transgender, queer, and other marginalized identities. It aims to create a safe and affirming learning environment for all students, regardless of their sexual orientation or gender identity, and to promote critical thinking and dialogue about social issues related to gender and sexuality. Queer pedagogy can involve incorporating queer themes and perspectives into course content, using inclusive language and terminology, creating opportunities for open discussion and reflection, and recognizing the diversity of identities and experiences within the classroom. Queer pedagogy is at the intersection of critical pedagogy and queer theory. It 'seeks to both uncover and disrupt hidden curricula of heteronormativity as well as to develop classroom landscapes and experiences that create safety for queer participants' (Thomas-Reid, 2018). Through the application of a queer pedagogy in a sexual health translation context, one not only disrupts knowledge, but also insists on challenging norms. Queerness is inherently transgressive and disruptive because it exposes the possibilities of sexualities (O'Driscoll, 1996). Queer pedagogy puts into practice what critical pedagogy has been postulating for years, that is, 'teaching students how not only to think but to come to grips with a sense of individual and social responsibility, and what it means to be responsible for one's actions as part of a broader attempt to be an engaged citizen who can expand and deepen the possibilities of democratic public life' (Giroux, 2013). It stands to critique mainstream education. The involvement of students in a live project that provides socially useful tools and information for sexual prevention represents the ultimate example of a critical approach to classroom life and reframes the classroom as a 'site of resistance' (McLaren, 2003, p. 78) by awakening students' critical consciousness and helping them transform their world (Freire, 1993) through a process of emancipation.

Queer pedagogy makes us stop and consider things outside of a normatively heterosexual gaze by encouraging alternative ways of knowing and being (where queerness itself can be associated with anti-assimilation politics). Consequently, we need queer theory because knowledge creation is always partial (Foucault, 1972), especially since our goal as educators should be to promote critical consciousness by using whatever method we have at our disposal. This is partially because it is true that everyone sees things differently, but also because what seems self-evident to one person may not be for another.

Queer theory has a place in sexual education whether or not we personally identify as LGBTQ+ because challenging dominant ideology using alternative perspectives (whether one agrees with them or not) is a beneficial act. Including queer perspectives allows educators to learn different ways of seeing things, which may include seeing things previously unseen at all. In many ways, it offers representation for people otherwise being ignored and wanting access to education on topics relevant to their life experiences in an effort to be heard.

It could be argued that queer pedagogy is, in essence, more about people rather than a specific methodology or technique. It is centred around the study object of its own analysis. It is a transformational approach about creating 'norm-exploding pedagogies, programmes and people who refuse to conform to erasures based on the pervasiveness of rigid normalising categories' (Quilty, 2017, p. 108). In order for this to happen, tutors must be committed to challenging the categories and topics which normally imbue academic syllabuses by allowing marginal voices and/or practices to be amplified, to take centre stage in a context which would otherwise prevent those voices from existing in traditional teaching, with the exception of dedicated originally queer-/gender-/feminist-oriented courses.

Queer pedagogy and queering pedagogy are therefore acts of courage and belief. They are about a hands-on commitment to equality and social justice, in a way. They provide an opportunity to conceive a different type of academia and permit students to participate in the creation of disruptive ways of going beyond academia (Quilty, 2017) simply by participating in such activities. Queer theory also plays a role in sexual health pedagogy because it inherently challenges heteronormativity and compulsory sexuality as normal. For many students, getting married or becoming parents is not necessarily a life goal; therefore, framing sexuality outside of traditional sexual reproduction narratives prevents them from being misinformed about sex. In queer theory, one of the primary goals is to challenge heteronormativity – that is, our conception of sexuality and sexual identity as normative. To do so, a postmodernist methodology could be employed that examines assumptions about heterosexuality in order to question them. In particular, we can look at how heteronormativity plays out in our sexual health curriculum. These kinds of interactions need to be debated critically in a global education classroom and open up opportunities for more inclusive discussions around safe sex practices. In the specific context of translation, it should be emphasized that translations always involve compromise and that different languages reach different audiences and goals across time (Fishman, 1991). Having an awareness of multiple viewpoints gives room for exploration and growth. While teaching is inherently political, if we do not examine ourselves critically, then it is hard to effect real change because doing so requires action on our part (both personally and professionally). It involves asking ourselves tough questions about the biases, beliefs, or assumptions we may have without feeling guilt or a fear of being labelled.

By simply bringing queerness into our classrooms and looking critically at how we teach students about sexuality (in translation) in a heteronormative world, anyone could find themselves empowered. Although in the context of the translation projects discussed here, the classroom is predominantly translation based and not centred around sexual education per se, these considerations extend and apply to the current context as well, as will be seen in the discussion of the translation projects that follows.

5 Localizing Sexual Health: Premise, Prospects, and Products

The projects in question involved second-year (Level 5) BA Translation students at London Metropolitan University (UK). The BA Translation course is centred around education and training with a strong emphasis on social justice as encapsulated in the university's Education for Social Justice Framework (ESJF).[2]

The projects being discussed as part of this Element took place in the 2019–20, 2020–1 and 2021–2 academic years following a collaboration with PrEPster/The Love Tank (2019–20, 2020–1) and, subsequently, Preptrack (2021–2).[3] Students were asked to translate multilingual sexual health campaigns as part of a simulated project management task provided for in module TR5057 'Managing translation'. In this module, students deal with aspects of managing the translation process from the perspective of various agents in the translation workflow. They cover the types of work available in the translation industry and what skills they need to develop in order to succeed, for example

---

[2] See www.londonmet.ac.uk/about/equity/centre-for-equity-and-inclusion/a-fair-outcomes-approach-to-teaching-and-learning/the-degree-awarding-gap/education-for-social-justice-framework/.

[3] The Love Tank is a not-for-profit community interest community (CIC) that promotes the health and wellbeing of underserved communities through education, capacity building, and research (The Love Tank, 2022); Preptrack is a not-for-profit that develops technology for sexual health (The Preptrack Foundation, 2020–2).

learning about the roles and procedures in the translation workflow cycle, evaluating their own professional and transferable skills, and identifying appropriate ways of developing these skills through continuing professional development (CPD).[4] Students are also exposed to issues related to professional responsibility and ethical standards in the various roles that they undertake. This module runs in the spring semester, for twelve weeks, and the simulated project management task takes place mid-semester.

Generally the module is structured in a way that favours *distributed practice* (Dunlosky et al., 2013) as a learning technique. Distributed practice learning implies 'a schedule of practice that spreads out study activities over time' (Dunlosky et al., 2013, p. 6), thus benefiting long-term retention as opposed to back-to-back learning. The topics covered in module TR5057 are the object of the final summative assessment, which is structured as a portfolio comprising three sections: a first section centred around CPD and students' career goals; a second section devoted to students' reflections on their experience of the simulated project management task (i.e. the task that will be explored in this Element); and a third section debating a case study on translation and professional ethics.

The twelve-week module's content is therefore structured into three parts, each part covering one of the above-mentioned areas. During each session, time is dedicated to revisiting concepts and ideas first developed in the previous week, so as to create a 'chain of thought'; by doing this, students have an opportunity to recall previously taught material and to delve into new materials gradually and smoothly, which facilitates learning and levels of information retention.

Across the years, students were tasked with the translation of grassroots organizations' multilingual sexual health campaigns for the web. The Association of Translation Companies (ATC) in the UK encourages and promotes language support for non-governmental organizations (NGOs), grassroots organizations, and charities as a way of 'decreasing language barriers' (ATC, 2022) and allowing these entities to both reach wider audiences and address a variety of needs. By collaborating with grassroots organizations, students are also taught and shown the value that translation can have as a humanitarian, high-impact social act. It reframes the act of translation as a non-commodity whose quality depends on close interaction with the client and is therefore dictated, as in most translation projects, by 'the degree to which it follows the agreed-upon specifications' (Durban & Melby, 2008, p. 4).

The projects effectively started in the 2017–8 academic year; however, at the time no formal data collection (survey responses) was recorded. At the

---

[4] See the module specifications in the university module catalogue: intranet.londonmet.ac.uk/module-catalogue/record.cfm?mc=TR5057.

beginning of the 2017 term, students were asked to translate a short video for the promotion of pre-exposure prophylaxis (PrEP), which at the time was still being trialled in the UK.[5] The work consisted of a few lines to be translated into Polish and Russian for an international audience. The following year no translation work was requested. Health initiatives have included, amongst others:

- the translation of a syphilis awareness campaign website[6]
- educating and agitating for PrEP access in England
- frequently asked questions about PrEP[7]
- a sexual health app to plan and manage PrEP[8]
- various updates to website sections

Due to the hypertextual nature of the source texts (mainly web based), the projects involved elements of web localization, which will be understood as 'the process of customizing an application, webpage, or website for a given culture or locale' (Microsoft, 2016) by adapting the user interface (UI) to the expectations of web users, both source and target ones. Localizing a multilingual project involves prior preparation work, on the part of both PMs and translators, and involves a series of steps ranging from preparing any reference material to providing specifications about file formats and tools to be used, to setting requirements for simultaneous delivery ('simship') (GTE Localize, 2022). In the case of the projects being discussed here, the original websites and the app, including their graphics, were already live and available for translators to navigate and localize. The webpages and app were also provided as reference materials so that students could make an informed decision about any content adaptation as a result of the relationship between the text and visual elements.

The main target audience was identified as being the UK population at large, including its non-English-speaking communities living in the country, and partner organizations abroad. Depending on the year and on student language availability, the languages offered in translation were English into Arabic, French, German, Italian, Polish, Portuguese, Romanian, Russian, and Spanish.

The overall word count for all projects was set at around 7,000+ words, including hashtags: the projects were translated using Microsoft Word and/or

---

[5] The term PrEP stands for pre-exposure HIV prophylaxis. It is a way of preventing HIV infection by taking a pill on an ongoing basis before sex and continued after sex (Team Prepster, 2022). The video, titled 'PrEP street talk', can be viewed at the following YouTube page: www.youtube.com/watch?v=7uuL9yXOdV0&t=28s.

[6] Long Time No Syphilis: www.longtimenosyph.info/.

[7] Prepster: prepster.info/faq/.

[8] Preptrack goes multi-lingual: https://preptrack.co.uk/blog/2022/08/preptrack-goes-multi-lingual/.

Microsoft Excel, and the tasks were performed as a simulated project management task where two agencies were created and in which each student took on the role of either project manager, terminologist, translator, or revisor, based on their language combination and their preference for the roles available. Any students translating into English either worked as revisors in their source language (for example, a student translating from French into English would revise the into-French translations) or they would put themselves forward to work as PMs, which was mostly the case in all projects. The roles were split by the students themselves once they met as an 'agency' for the first time, and the role of the tutor was to randomly assign students to each agency bearing in mind the availability of language combinations. As a further quality control step, it was decided to also appoint senior revisors, that is, students from the university's master's degree in translation or senior BA students that had been previously involved in the project, to ensure the utmost quality via their translation experience and knowledge of the subject matter. Although this seemingly 'rudimental' implementation of a further quality control step does not fully reflect comprehensive and agile processes adopted in a standard localization workflow, involving target-language speakers as an additional step to ensure compliance with local norms and conventions reflects the fluid nature of the localization quality workflow, deemed as necessary to avoid the potential rejection of the final product on the part of the target users/consumers (Mitchell-Schuitevoerder, 2020).

In the week prior to the start of the project, students were introduced to the concepts and practice of *queer translation* and *queering* as an academic exercise. Up until that point, no other translation module or syllabus of the BA Translation course had specifically covered these two topics and, following in-class discussions with the students, it was understood that the only context in which most students had heard the word *queer* until then was as a slur, although some of them ignored this meaning too. As such, it was explained how *queer* had become an umbrella term for non-normative identities, practices, and sexualities, as well as a reclaimed term.

The following definitions were therefore provided as a basis for the contextualization of the tasks to be conducted but also as shared knowledge from which to start a debate:

- *Queering*: a method that can be applied to literature as well as film to look for places where things such as gender, sexuality, masculinity, and femininity can be challenged and questioned (Barker & Scheele, 2016; Warner, 1993).
- *Queer translation*: a critique of sexuality and translation as categories which are interrogated through the dual process of translating sexuality and the sexualization of translation (Kedem, 2019).

Students were first asked what their understanding of these concepts was and whether they felt that they were equipped with the right tools and knowledge to deliver the products in alignment with these frameworks. In general, it was understood that although students did not know the details of how to effectively 'queer' a text or a product, they showed a strong willingness to be guided and to learn.

After introducing the students to the above definitions, they were presented with an outline of the projects, detailing information about the commissioner, file formats and content, the suggested deadlines, and the language combinations required. The latter varied according to cohort and type of project and, as detailed earlier, they were mainly texts and materials to be translated from English into other languages. Finally, the tutor invited students to ask and prepare preliminary questions about the project before meeting the client the following week. This was done so as to provide a safe space for students to ask any questions that they might have considered inappropriate or 'too basic' for the client. It was noted that the fact that they were expected to meet a real client and interact with them put them under pressure of wanting to look competent and professional, and to ask the right questions. What was observed during this preliminary meeting was that students asked very pertinent questions regarding the project workflow: for example, when the files were due to be sent by the client; which computer-aided-translation (CAT) tools they were supposed to use; how they would split the translation agencies; and who would be in charge of what. The meeting generally showcased the translation knowledge learnt up until that point.[9] Very little was asked in relation to the practical aspects of *queering*, apart from questioning the availability of collateral materials (translations or original materials) about sexual health in their respective languages, a common concern which was also shared in the surveys that they were invited to fill in at the end of each project and which will be discussed in Section 6.

Meeting the client before the start of a project is deemed a key step in good project management practices (Matis, 2017). For all projects, one of the founders of The Love Tank and PrEPster came to visit us, both pre-pandemic and once students returned on campus after the pandemic. In the 2022 meet-the-client session, he was joined by the founder of the sexual health app Preptrack, which was also translated by the students. During these preliminary meetings, the students had the opportunity to request further information about the

---

[9] CAT tools are software programs used to aid the translation process by providing a variety of components (translation memory, i.e. a database that stores source sentences and their translations; termbase, i.e. a terminology database for storing terms and expressions; machine translation; dictionaries, etc.) to speed up the translation process and enhance quality (RWS Trados, n.d.).

projects and learn about any specific requirements, such as the use of inclusive language and preference for language variation: for example, for the Portuguese copy, they were asked to produce a copy that would work internationally, seeing as the content of the website was also used by both Brazilian and Portuguese organizations. A similar request was made for the Arabic version which, although required for a UK audience, was expected to be used by partner organizations in the Middle East too. These localization decisions were made on the basis of web user statistics produced by The Love Tank but also in response to web visitors' views once a first set of translations was released in the earlier projects. The statistics provided in Figure 1 cover web traffic from 2019 onwards and uncover a revealing picture of how web localization can drive user traffic and localization efforts.

Although they were not provided as an indicator of web usability, and thus an analysis of this will not be presented here, the statistics produced by The Love Tank showed the pre-translation web user traffic (2019) and the post-translation /localization traffic (2022). In the 2019 statistics, monolingual UK users made up the majority of visitors to the website, followed by a minority of EU and non-EU countries totalling users in the hundreds out of a total of 5,595 visitors.

	5,595 % of Total 100.00% (5,595)		18,424 % of Total 100.00% (18,424)
1. United Kingdom	2,209 (39.36%)	1. United Kingdom	7,511 (41.02%)
2. Brazil	682 (12.15%)	2. Japan	3,301 (18.03%)
3. United States	510 (9.09%)	3. Saudi Arabia	1,037 (5.66%)
4. Italy	462 (8.23%)	4. Italy	583 (3.18%)
5. Spain	426 (7.59%)	5. Brazil	455 (2.48%)
6. Poland	193 (3.44%)	6. United States	448 (2.45%)
7. Germany	115 (2.05%)	7. Jordan	407 (2.22%)
8. France	91 (1.62%)	8. Egypt	390 (2.13%)
9. Australia	66 (1.18%)	9. Poland	349 (1.91%)
10. Canada	47 (0.84%)	10. Spain	318 (1.74%)
11. Netherlands	47 (0.84%)	11. India	212 (1.16%)
12. Bulgaria	44 (0.78%)	12. Germany	207 (1.13%)
13. Switzerland	38 (0.68%)	13. Algeria	186 (1.02%)
14. Ireland	37 (0.66%)	14. Lebanon	164 (0.90%)
15. India	36 (0.64%)	15. Iraq	162 (0.88%)
16. Singapore	27 (0.48%)	16. Libya	150 (0.82%)
17. Japan	26 (0.46%)	17. France	130 (0.71%)
2019		2022	

Figure 1 PrEPster/The Love Tank web traffic – 2019 versus 2022 (as at 21 February 2022).

Compared to the 2022 statistics, the total number of visitors appeared to have more than trebled, with UK users making up more than 40 per cent of the total, and all other countries racking up hundreds of users each. The UK figure could be explained if we consider that The Love Tank webpages appeared in translation after 2019, thus providing multilingual communities in the UK access to their own language versions of the websites. In a way, this testifies to the nature of localization as a vessel for democratic interaction spurred by multilingualism (Pym, 2011) and reflected in user traffic. It is striking how the website registered a wider presence of Arabic-speaking countries/users in the 2022 list, which could be explained by the availability of sexual health content in Arabic in countries where traditionally sexual health content is rarely other than heterocentric. In the other countries in the list (e.g. Italy, Poland, Germany, France) and whose languages were offered in translation, a sensible increase in the number of web users can also be seen, which further proves the reach and scope of the newly translated content.

In most mainstream translation projects, translators act as 'mediating agents, reading a source text as a first step before opting for one of the various (though not unlimited) possible readings and deciding the best way of rewriting their understanding of the text' (Castro, 2013, p. 39). Unlike mainstream translation projects, the peculiarity of the projects being explored in this Element is that the source text was already written using inclusive language, and this is because the main client – The Love Tank – is a grassroots organization working closely with a wide spectrum of communities, including underrepresented minorities in sexual health. Therefore the novelty effect was that the product was already 'queered' at source, de facto stripping the source of any ambiguity or bias in the original text which could have been replicated in the translation and could have uncovered potential bias on the part of the translator (Ghazala, 2002). This means that the source text was formulated in a way that already honoured and took into consideration non-heterocentric/heteronormative practices and realities which, as a result, were expected to be reproduced in translation too. As an analogy between localization steps and queering translation steps, the concept of internationalization can prove useful at this point: internationalization means neutralizing content, code, and design in a product so that the product can then be adapted easily to any type of culture or target language for which it is intended (Bodrov-Krukowski, 2020). With the culture-specific elements removed from the internationalized version, the site tends to remain 'within functionalist technical culture' (Pym, 2011, p. 276), which may be associated with the client in question, thereby creating the illusion of a technological world without culture as a result of the ideology of internationalization. The use of non-sexist language in the source text represented an ideological stance and a product-intrinsic characteristic that the student-translators were asked to adhere to as part of the client's brief: the 'compendium of the function of the translation and its context of reception' (Jiménez-Crespo, 2009) and the project's *skopos*, that is, the ultimate purpose of the target text (Nord, 2022), which are the cornerstones of functionalism in translation. As pointed out by Castro (2013b, p. 38), 'applying linguistic strategies for a non-sexist use of language in translations could entirely (or mostly) depend on (the translator's interpretation of) the gender ideologies conveyed in the source text, or on (the translator's interpretation of) the purpose or *skopos* of the target text'.

In this case, the *skopos* was to cater for as multiculturally and multilinguistically varied a population as possible. In particular, the language used in translation must take into account the original commissioner's requirement for inclusive, non-binary language as well as target-culture and language sensitivities, thus effectively queering translation, that is, contesting existing knowledge production (Spurlin, 2014b). As already mentioned, this approach has been found to bridge the gap in multicultural health promotion uncovered by Ji and colleagues (2020), who lament the fact that the lack of provision of multilingual sex content becomes more costly to sustain due to poor knowledge and resources on the part of the potential target audience. It also meets the needs of a multicultural user base by addressing its demographic variability (Ji et al., 2020). Once again, translation as a whole can be considered as an opportunity to showcase the delicate balance between opposing needs and the tensions actualized in the final product as a result of the ultimate functional purpose of the target text.

In the projects being analysed, translation was proactively employed to promote sexual health and to make it more accessible via inclusive and accessible language (Ji, 2020). This can be interpreted as a form of social activism, where language is used to disseminate information across marginalized communities, thus overcoming structural, systemic hindrances. Translation as a whole can therefore be seen as a social vessel for change (De Marco & Toto, 2019): this implies actively taking a stance in the face of ethical, social, and ideological triggers in order to elaborate 'gender-positive and queer-positive productions of meaning' (De Marco & Toto, 2019, p. 192), as well as accountability for the translator's intermediation. It is crucial that students and translation tutors develop an awareness of their position in society and realize how their actions can contribute to demystifying or creating barriers. This awareness will be explored in Section 6 through the findings of the survey that was run in response to the projects.

As a pedagogical tool and when applied to these particular projects, translation relied on the concept of *pedagogy of discomfort*, a term coined by Boler in

1999, which involves students being challenged in terms of their preconceived notions and biases. A pedagogy of discomfort presents students with situations that challenge their knowledge and it encourages, among other things, both self-reflection on their part and a call to action (Boler, 1999) whose aims are to trigger change in society and a change in relation to students' societal role.

Pedagogical translation that opens up to a queer view of the act of translation itself embeds queer pedagogy: this means multiplying the possibilities of knowledge, starting from ignorance as a form of knowledge itself (Shlasko, 2005). Queering pedagogy within a context of 'discomfort' also means pushing the boundaries of what is considered normal in speech acts; it works at the intersection of normalcy, that is, the production of normalcy. It is 'teaching against the grain', that is, going against the mainstream curriculum, which involves raising questions about students' role in society and how translators can disrupt binary conceptions of sexual health and its associated language. One way of doing this is by providing students with materials that do not reinforce the binary normalcy exception, but rather make normalcy the exception instead. Students were therefore involved in projects that can be ascribed to both queer translation, that is, projects which foreground translation as a form of social activism, and to embedding queer pedagogy.

At the end of the project, approximately a month and a half after the first meeting with the client, students were asked to rate and discuss their experience according to set criteria. To gauge this, an anonymous online survey was administered via Google Forms, which will be covered in the next section.

6 Querying Approaches to Sexual Health Translation: Survey and Data

Throughout the years of the projects, a total of sixty-four students took part in the projects and a total of thirty-nine students (i.e. more than half) filled in the final surveys at the end of the projects. In terms of demographics, the majority of respondents comprised predominantly white, self-declared cis, straight females having no disability, and mostly EU or UK natives; less than 3 per cent of the overall number of respondents identified as queer or as other. This information was anonymously derived from other data-gathering survey-type documents issued by the university itself and circulated as part of the module in question.

At this stage it is necessary to point out that the individual language solutions in the translations were not assessed on this occasion and that the survey was not meant to investigate the reasons for choosing specific translation solutions. The purpose of the survey was to determine the overall experience of the students when confronted with sexual health content and whether they felt equipped to tackle the task on the basis of their existing knowledge of sexual-health-related matters and terminology. As part of the project-based assignments, the survey purported to be an opportunity for (self-)reflection and analysis as well as a final evaluation of the collaborative task (Mitchell-Schuitevoerder, 2020). As such, from a methodological point of view and considering however that queer theories 'do not espouse any particular methodology applicable to the study of language' (Sauntson, 2008, p. 272), the analysis of the data follows a phenomenological qualitative method that 'allows to track empathy and recognition of both the researcher's and the participant's subjectivity in relation to the phenomenon being explored' (Alhazmi & Kaufmann, 2022). The focus of the ensuing analysis will be the interpretation of meanings in both a collective and subjective experience, thus highlighting the empirical and observational nature of this case study. Empiricism and observational analysis are often used in translation studies to test a methodology or a hypothesis, to investigate the translator's working procedures, or to answer translation-related questions, such as the effectiveness of quality workflows or the outcome of specific processes (Williams & Chesterman, 2002). The case study explored here can be attributed to the latter kind of research whereby qualitative data analysis will identify, evaluate, and offer an interpretation of patterns and themes in the data.

Data will be reproduced and interpreted from the last three cohorts participating in the projects, namely from 2019–20, 2020–1 and 2021–2. The charts will also indicate the number of responses per question to provide concrete evdence of student engagement. The data being analysed does not include the early 2017 video project as no proper data collection was performed then, only a post-mortem anonymous evaluation via Padlet,[10] which, however can be considered as statistically and qualitatively negligible.

The first question was about how confident students felt while translating the text in terms of familiarity with the subject matter, that is, whether they had any knowledge about STIs and whether they knew their equivalents in their respective target languages. Although formulated predominantly for students acting as translators, the question was left open for interpretation to those involved in proofreading too, whereas it did not overtly cover students acting as PMs, which in hindsight may be considered as a limitation of the scope of the survey.

Students could choose among the options displayed in Figures 2 to 4. Across the three academic years in question, the overwhelming majority indicated that they felt 'very confident' or 'confident' in terms of familiarity with the subject matter, with only about one-third of students feeling 'somewhat confident' instead. Only in

---

[10] In localization studies, this corresponds to a project review after its completion to collect client feedback and consider any lessons learned.

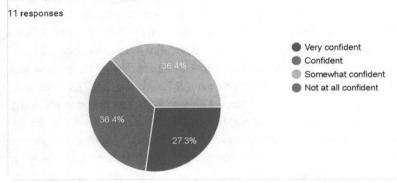

Figure 2 Results from the 2019–20 survey, Question 1.

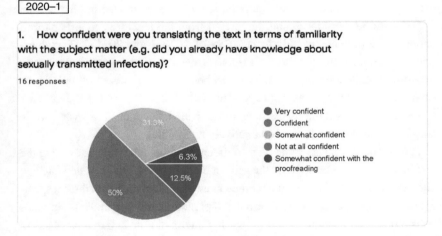

Figure 3 Results from the 2020–1 survey, Question 1.

the last academic year's survey did a small number of students (two out of the twelve respondents, to be precise) feel 'not at all confident'. This, however, should not necessarily be interpreted as a negative indicator of the overall experience, as will be gauged from the analysis of the qualitative feedback in Section 7.

When asked to elaborate on the level of confidence/comfort experienced when translating sexual-health-related materials (Question 2), the comments partially reproduced in Table 1 were made. For methodological purposes the

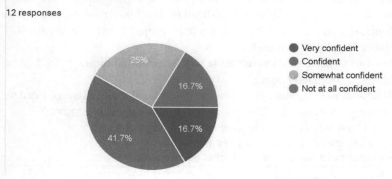

2021–2

1. How confident were you translating the text in terms of familiarity with the subject matter (e.g. did you already have knowledge about sexually transmitted infections)?

12 responses

- Very confident
- Confident
- Somewhat confident
- Not at all confident

25%

16.7%

16.7%

41.7%

Figure 4 Results from the 2021–2 survey, Question 1.

comments are presented in table form, as representative samples (without altering their content), and grammatically edited. It should be noted that, for the sake of transparency and for a full appreciation of the qualitative nature of the results obtained, an Appendix has been provided with the complete and unabridged sets of responses received from all the cohorts. In this way, the students' tone, register, and enthusiasm about the project or lack thereof can be fully appreciated and independently evaluated in an unfiltered manner.

In the tables that follow, comments from all years have been coded, grouped, and classified based on three main categories: Positive, Neutral/Mixed, and Pessimistic. Positive comments explicitly commend the experience and provide a constructive evaluation of it; Neutral/Mixed comments indicate that the respondent showed mixed feelings about the experience (e.g. they enjoyed some aspects of it but were stifled in others) or indicate that it was not possible to clearly classify the 'mood' of the comment; finally, Pessimistic (rather than negative) comments indicate that the respondent was 'on the fence' or showed uncertainty about their own experience (but not the task itself, as will be shown). Any duplicate/repeated comments in any category have been omitted. Furthermore, comments have been revised for legibility without altering their content. For the purpose of further discussion, some key themes in the comments have been highlighted in bold in all the tables to show patterns of responses:

Analysing these comments, the majority of answers confirm the positive impact of this experience, showing some level of enthusiasm and a certain degree of positivity towards the tasks. As mentioned earlier, the selected responses

Table 1 Students' comments in relation to Question 1.

Positive Comments

- I felt **comfortable** as I already knew a little bit about the subject.
- I was **completely at ease** with the content.
- I felt **comfortable** translating sexual-health-related materials, despite my unfamiliarity with the topic[;] throughout the project I was able to **educate** not just others but also myself about it.
- I have always been **very comfortable with sex-related topics**, since I grew up with open-minded parents.
- I **felt confident** translating sexual-health-related materials, although I had to educate myself to acquire further knowledge about the subject matter.
- I did not have any concerns in terms of the topic of the text.
- Yes, **no difference to any other translation**.
- **The content did not affect my moral convictions.**

Neutral/Mixed Comments

- Having done the glossary, I felt comfortable with the topic itself. **Nevertheless**, a few terms were very specific to the medical field and required a lot more time to find the pertinent TL equivalent, especially when not inserted in a context.[11]
- The subject matter was quite new to me and I was **anxious** about translating it. **However** . . . it became interesting and motivating . . . .
- **Although** it is not very easy to talk about **sexual health issues in my culture**, this project's audience was UK based, so I was quite comfortable with it.
- I had never translated anything like this before, so I was **afraid of making a mistake** . . ..
- I felt a little bit **uncomfortable because I don't totally agree with [the] LGBTQ community**. However, **I wanted to challenge myself and prove that I can be professional** and to expand my knowledge.

Pessimistic Comments

- . . . **some terms I was not comfortable** to translate . . . .
- [on reviewing the text] it made me feel **a little uneasy** that people have to do this in order to have a sexual relationship with people.

represent the overall 'mood' of the cohorts and, as can be seen from the parts in bold, which will be further analysed in Section 7, students' attitudes varied sensibly: from feeling comfortable translating the content to purporting that sexual health was nothing to be ashamed about, to expressing feelings of uneasiness around some of the terms. The latter in particular is thought to refer to one

---

[11] The abbreviation TL refers to 'target language'.

specific website translated during the 2020–1 academic year, which dealt with syphilis prevention and which explicitly mentioned sexual practices which could be considered as 'niche', such as fisting or rimming. This is also potentially confirmed by one of the comments where a student said that while reviewing their text – and therefore it can be assumed that they were performing the role of proofreader – it made them feel 'a little uneasy that people have to do this in order to have a sexual relationship with others'. Although not statistically representative, this comment reveals particular cultural attitudes towards non-reproductive sexual practices and a trigger for this particular student.

In the next question, students were asked whether they felt equipped to translate the text in terms of lexical and real-world knowledge, and they were asked to specify whether they already knew the specialist terms included in the glossary provided to them by the tutor and/or whether they were already familiar with the relevant equivalents in their target language. Their answers are shown in Figures 5, 6 and 7.

In the first two academic years, only a small proportion of students felt 'fully equipped' to translate the terms based on their own real-world knowledge, whereas a large majority of them oscillated between 'somewhat equipped' and 'equipped'. In the third year, however, one-quarter of students felt 'fully equipped' from the onset, and another quarter responded that they felt 'equipped', bringing this to half of the cohort population being in a favourable and confident position at the start of the project as a result of

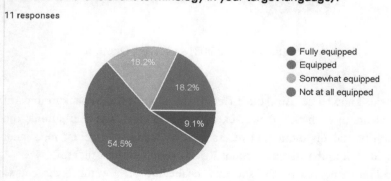

2019–20

3. How equipped did you feel you were to translate the text in terms of lexical and real-world knowledge (i.e. did you already know the specialist terms highlighted by the tutor in the source text; were you already familiar with the relevant terminology in your target language)?

11 responses

- Fully equipped
- Equipped
- Somewhat equipped
- Not at all equipped

18.2%
18.2%
9.1%
54.5%

Figure 5 Results from the 2019–20 survey, Question 3.

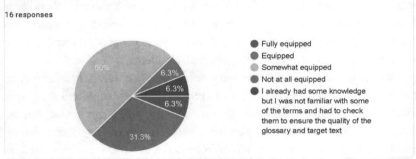

Figure 6 Results from the 2020–1 survey, Question 3.

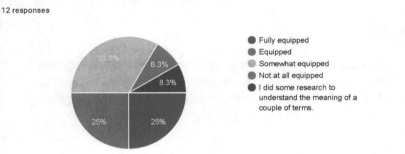

Figure 7 Results from the 2021–2 survey, Question 3.

their prior knowledge. Here the different social and cultural backgrounds of the students in each cohort may explain these percentage oscillations: the availability and dissemination of, as well as students' interest in, sexual health content in the students' countries of origin – or lack thereof.

Question 4 focused on the students' evaluation of how much the course prepared them for this type of translation task, on the basis of their experience of translation in general and of their specific translation course. They were asked to rate their experience using a slider from 1 to 5, with 1 being 'I was completely unprepared to translate sexual-health-related content, i.e. inclusive language terminology register, etc.' and 5 being 'The translation course fully prepared me to translate sexual-health-related content':

Across the years, there was a strong indication that students felt that the course had prepared them fairly well for the task at hand, as can be seen from the percentages shown in Figures 9–11.

As can be seen from focusing on the upper end of all of the scales, the overwhelming majority of respondents indicated that they considered the translation course as having fully prepared them or mostly prepared them to translate the relevant sexual health content. Their answers are shown in Figure 8. Only about 10 per cent of all respondents on aggregate indicated that the course had not prepared them for the task.

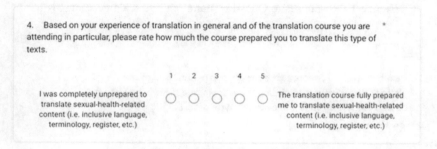

Figure 8 Question 4 and the option scale.

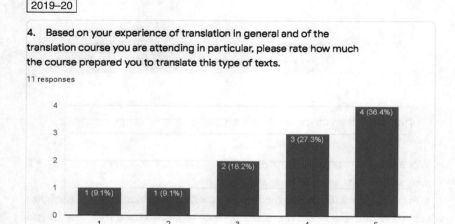

Figure 9 Responses to Question 4 and relative scale percentages.

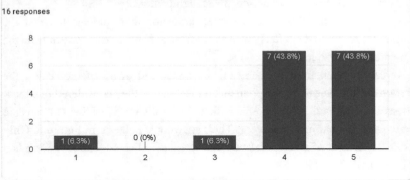

Figure 10 Responses to Question 4 and relative scale percentages.

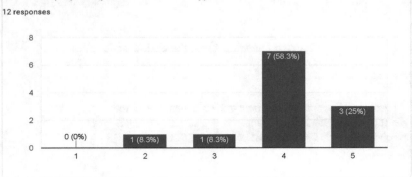

Figure 11 Responses to Question 4 and relative scale percentages.

When asked to elaborate further on these answers, the comments in Table 2 were made (shown as a representative selection).

As is common with course/module evaluation forms across the UK higher education sector, that is, the forms students are requested to complete at the end of each term to gauge their satisfaction in terms of course/module content, teaching, facilities, and so on (Murray & Smith, 2013), the points raised by the

Table 2 Students' comments in relation to Question 4.

Positive Comments

- Although it is not a topic we discuss on a daily basis, I feel like I was prepared to perform this task as my tutor [gave] me enough **guidance** to perform this . . ..
- The course has provided me with **translation strategies** to deal with the implementation of inclusive language, even in my target language. I have learned how to get to the right **resources** I would obtain my **terminology** from, and also how to identify when a formal/informal **register** is needed. I have been taught about **ethics in translation**, meeting the deadlines and making sure you provide a good-quality translation.
- The course prepared us well to be ready to translate sexual health content.
- The course has prepared me to translate sexual-health-related content as I have been taught how to use inclusive language . . ..
- The course prepared me very well.
- The course fully prepared me to translate sexual-health-related content.
- I was **aware of [language inclusivity]** from previous seminars and I was equipped with the skills to target my research and approach the task.
- The course fully prepared me to engage with specific different areas.
- The course has provided me with knowledge of register and adaptation of the language in context. It trained me on how to best adhere to the [client's] requirements, to adapt the language according to **the brief**, function, intention and target audience and to make the most appropriate decisions.
- I did a community interpreting course in the past and have been working as an interpreter ever since, which is more or less quite similar to my current translation course; however the amount of **tools and experience** that I have learnt since the start of the course is amazing and it helped me to work on this project.
- We widely discussed how important it is to identify the **needs of the client** and what type of target text is expected, what the audience would be and other important aspects . . . . We also talked about the market so I already felt prepared in that aspect.
- **The [module] leader** has made everything easy for us as students, I was fully prepared and was fully aware of the content and how important [it is] to use inclusive language, terminology and register, especially the fact that the people in charge of the app came to see us in person . . ..

Neutral/Mixed Comments

- **We had never had a chance to translate something sexual-health-related before. However,** the vocabulary was not an issue, as we managed to find everything using parallel texts and dictionaries. The real challenge was keeping the information easy to understand for a wide audience, with such a **delicate topic**, and keeping the language informal and gender neutral.

Table 2 (cont.)

During the translation course, especially thanks to the language-specific sessions, we were prepared to face and solve these problems professionally.
- They keep the course and the documents we have to translate **quite general**. This was the first time for me to translate a sexual-health-related text **but** I enjoyed it.
- The course I am attending pretty much covers all aspects and topics in translation but in regard to sexual-health-related content I believe that **there has not been much time invested** in these. But **the lecturer has definitely been very present** in guiding and providing us with feedback throughout the project whenever needed.
- This course gives me the necessary **tools and knowledge** for the translation activity. **However,** I was not prepared to carry out a translation on sexual-health-related content.
- **We did not touch on inclusive language in depth. However,** we were taught how to research and find reliable sources which could replace the lack of inclusive language training.
- Through the lectures on the translation process and procedures, I learnt how to deal with specific issues related to culture and other types including gender. **However,** I am still **not very familiar with non-binary gender approaches** in translation into my target language (French). I realized a real gap in my knowledge of how much things are evolving in that respect.
- We discussed [it] in some of the previous subjects but not in an extensive way, I would say. I feel like I have obtained a lot more knowledge about inclusive language from my own experience and research on the internet, but then again, it is something that interests me personally.

Pessimistic Comments

- To begin with, I firmly believe that we should work more on inclusive translation. Most languages we translate into are very different from English in terms of gender, which can make it difficult to produce inclusive translations. Regarding terminology, maybe we were not familiarised with sexual-health-related terms, but the course prepared us to be able to find reliable sources to consult the terms.
- We did very **few lessons on "how to queer our language"**.

students may be in conflict with one another (for example, 'The course prepared me very well' versus 'The course did not provide me with all the necessary tools' in the comments for the same cohort), which may complicate the interpretation of the data in terms of any action plans to be taken in order to address any perceived deficits in the delivery of the course/module. Based on a purely quantitative appreciation of the comments provided in the surveys being evaluated in this section and listed under each header in Table 2, it is possible to deduce that, as far as the course preparing the students for the projects in question is concerned, the overwhelming majority expressed itself in a positive manner, with only a very small minority indicating the opposite.

The final question in the survey related to how easy it was for students to find suitable material in their target language (resources/websites to consult in order to find the equivalents) that could be used as a reference corpus. Their answers are shown in Figures 12, 13 and 14. Although the majority of the combined responses indicated that research was between 'somewhat easy' and 'very easy', a small percentage of students indicated that it was tricky to find resources in their own target language because they could not find that many materials about sexual health or did not know where to locate them online.

In this instance, 58 per cent of students out of the thirty-nine respondents replied that it was either 'very easy' or 'easy' and 30 per cent of them replied that it was 'somewhat easy' to find suitable material; only 5 per cent of respondents struggled to find suitable parallel texts and therefore stated that it was 'not at all easy'.

Finally, students were asked to comment on their experience of working on the translation, highlighting in particular which elements they found

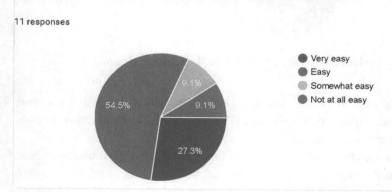

2019–20

5. How easy was it for you to find suitable material in your target language to use as corpus (i.e. did you already know which resources/websites to consult in order to find suitable parallel texts)?

11 responses

- Very easy
- Easy
- Somewhat easy
- Not at all easy

54.5%
9.1%
9.1%
27.3%

Figure 12 Results from the 2019–20 survey, Question 5.

5. How easy was it for you to find suitable material in your target language to use as corpus (i.e. did you already know which resources/websites to consult in order to find suitable parallel texts)?

16 responses

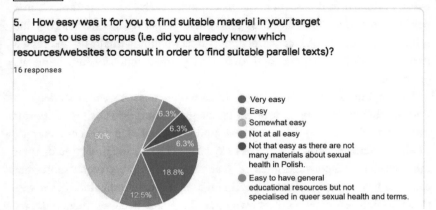

Figure 13 Results from the 2020–1 survey, Question 5.

2021–2

5. How easy was it for you to find suitable material in your target language to use as corpus (i.e. did you already know which resources/websites to consult in order to find suitable parallel texts)?

12 responses

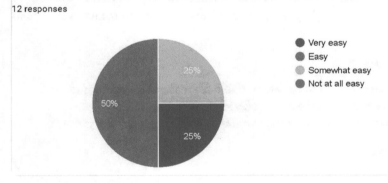

Figure 14 Results from the 2021–2 survey, Question 5.

challenging, and which ones enjoyable or tangibly different from other translation tasks. Table 3 shows a selection of the comments made (shown as a representative sample).

Overall student feedback regarding this point was very positive apart from a couple of comments which stated that the students did not think that they had been prepared as best as they could for the translation of sexual-related content. It can be appreciated that in some cases students struggled to find suitable

Table 3 Students' comments in relation to Question 6.

Positive Comments

- It was an enjoyable and a very interesting translation to do.
- I enjoyed working for this translation since I think **the cause is important**.
- I enjoyed working on this project and appreciate the **work dynamics** monitoring by the PMs.
- It was an inspiring experience in terms of the importance of translators as activists. Language should be up to date with the society and the **current variety of gender identities**.
- It was enjoyable and constructive. It fulfilled me with insight on **what happens behind a translation project**, the various roles and expectations . . ..
- It is great to be part of a project that will have a **significant social impact**.
- **Meeting the client** and getting to know the project and the website have definitely been a plus. . . . I have also enjoyed **learning more about sexual health** and prevention . . ..
- My overall experience was insightful, as it helped me discover how delicate it is to deal with gender bias in texts . . ..
- This experience was surely different from other experiences I had in the past as it brought **the feel of the real word** into it!
- Personally, it was [quite an enjoyable] experience because I am really interested in gender-inclusive translation and this was a great opportunity to practise my previously acquired skills.
- I think it is vital to normalise the discussion about STIs and sexual health in general since it still seems to be taboo in some environments. I am also happy since I've never had an opportunity to translate materials around this topic, so for me it was an invaluable experience.
- . . . the purpose of this collaboration has inspired me personally: I realised more that **the work of a translator is always valuable** and also that from small to big translations the final product will somehow always have an **impact on the reader**.
- It was a great experience in terms of communication and cooperation as a team to complete the project.
- Hope to take on more similar projects.

Neutral/Mixed Comments

- . . . It surely **took me out of my comfort zone** in terms of working as a team but the overall experience has been constructive. . . . I found combining gender-neutral and informal language with such delicate information challenging. . . . **lowering the register without affecting the readability** of the text and the clarity of information was difficult at times.

Table 3 (cont.)

- I found the review of the translation hard as I had to **review in my foreign language** and so **I wasn't too sure** about the grammatical rules in the language. I was a little apprehensive to change anything other than some words that I knew could be written a little better for the overall flow and **space constraints of the text**.
- … What I realised is that in my target language they talk about syphilis **but not as explicitly** and detailed and direct as in this project … .
- I enjoyed the overall experience. **However**, the role of proofreading I didn't enjoy too much … issues appeared and the level of anxiety was very high.
- Overall it was a really good experience as it represented a real-life scenarios. … .. **However**, it did make me realise that probably working individually in a project such as this one would have been easier for stylistic and consistency reasons. It was really interesting and enhanced my interest in localisation.
- I did enjoy the topic because it's a topic I like and I already know about; I found it **challenging working with people that had close to zero knowledge** about that.
- The **tricky part** has been with the terminology, because in my language there is no corpus, glossary or anything like that. … .. However, in my country there is a lot of talk about sexual diseases, so I have been able to consult different websites, such as the one of the government of my country, which talk openly about the subject. The problem is that the terminology varies a lot from one site to another and I have had to make decisions about it.

Pessimistic Comments

- There were some difficulties in **finding parallel texts** into some of the languages we have provided … .
- … I couldn't find a correct translation for some terminology … **It was really hard.**
- There were **not many parallel texts** online.
- The project was really **challenging** because I was not fully familiar with the terms.
- The hardest part of the project was **to fit it in my schedule**.
- The project was **really challenging** because I was not fully familiarized with the terms.

equivalent material or to adhere to constraints dictated by writing for the web. Overall, though, they stated that it was a pleasant experience that made them realize how important their role was both within the overall translation process and from a social-impact point of view. There was also a distinct educational element in the experience which came out in the comments: students admitted to learning more about sexual health and therefore getting an education from it. In their own words, it took them out of their comfort zone.

Overall, the surveys show that a dual process happens when translation trainees are faced with this type of content: firstly, for them it is a matter of understanding how *queering* a product works when expressly requested by their commissioner, which will require investigating where the product might need neutralizing and being more inclusive; secondly, it is about queering the agents of translation and translators' agency, which means outlining how translators can be involved in the changes that need to happen at more structural levels, as will be discussed in the next concluding section.

7 Querying Translation Products and Agents

Among the themes emerging from the surveys, some clear patterns can be identified. In the students' comments in relation to Question 1, the positive comments highlighted a pre-existing interest in or background knowledge of sexual health. The representative sample shown indicates that only a very small minority of students felt 'uncomfortable' translating the content provided to them. This was mainly due to the fact that the students in question were possibly confronted with new lived-experience situations and language which they felt unprepared to deal with, which allowed them to conceptualize their relationships in a different manner (Bryson & De Castell, 1993). Although in a real-life situation (freelance) translators may decline jobs which pose an ethical dilemma or which they simply do not wish to carry out, in the context proposed this option was not available: all students were supposed and expected to take part in the project or risked failing the module altogether. Students were expected to adhere to the *skopos* of the projects and while this may be misconstrued as an enforcement of functionalist translation principles, it was presented as an opportunity to engage, possibly for the first time ever, with an actual client and to have their work published online.[12] It also represented an opportunity for them to play a significant role in a safe environment (the classroom).

As part of the neutral comments, what transpired was a perceived inadequacy at managing terminology requirements or the task itself, with an added component of slight apprehension at having to lend their voice to causes with which

---

[12] The materials provided were part of a national prevention campaign whose successful implementation has resulted, together with other nationally directed campaigns, in a drop in HIV rates in the UK following PrEP use to 2,955 new HIV diagnoses in the UK in 2021 (0.2 percent down on 2020; 33 percent up on 2019). See *HIV testing, PrEP, new HIV diagnoses, and care outcomes for people accessing HIV services: 2022 report*, available at www.gov.uk/government/statistics/hiv-annual-data-tables/hiv-testing-prep-new-hiv-diagnoses-and-care-outcomes-for-people-accessing-hiv-services-2022-report.

they did not feel 100 per cent aligned. This uneasiness was also reflected in the limited pessimistic comments provided, which revealed personal attitudes towards sex positivity and unfamiliarity with sexual practices.

When analysing students' preparedness for the task, their comments in relation to Question 4 showed that they resorted to their existing translation knowledge in order to deal with the more practical aspects of the projects. They also stressed the professional and 'real-world' feel of the task, which possibly spurred them on and provided the motivation they needed to complete the task. This would point towards the importance of scaffolding knowledge (Marshall et al., 2014), which is a key element, especially in the undergraduate higher education curriculum. Students valued the course syllabus and tried to showcase their own expertise by making explicit reference to topics and issues covered as part of their programme (e.g. register, ethics in translation, the client's brief). This, however, was not unanimously supported when looking at the neutral and pessimistic comments; in fact, a handful of students expressed their disappointment at not having covered these topics more in depth or earlier in the academic year, but admitted nevertheless that it was a constructive experience for them, which may be interpreted as an indication of interest towards this aspect of their experience.

It is, however, in their responses in relation to their experience of working on the translations that the complete spectrum of their comments can be fully appreciated: as can be seen, Table 3 is the only table where the comments balance each other out and present a mixture of points to be considered across the three categories, ranging from technical translation aspects to the obstacles encountered during the translation process, to the challenges encountered, which were mainly of a procedural/workflow-related nature rather than topic related.

A common denominator in the comments is the focus on the practical task rather than on the disruption potentially caused by the subject matter. Due to its formative nature and its potential for professional recognition, the task presumably allowed students to temporarily suspend any (moral) judgement in relation to the topics being covered, thus enabling them to concentrate only on the final delivery of the products.

A significant point that emerged from the surveys was the educational value of this experience: not only did students learn about STIs and sexual practices, but they also learned about the power of language and the difference that it can make to minority communities. This case study also showed the necessity to challenge students' bias as well as that of the educators – and in particular the queer educator – to refrain from promoting their own agenda (Elder, 1999; Kopelson, 2002), which is a real potential issue when queering translation. It could be argued that the students' response to the task may have been affected by the lecturer's commitment to gender concerns and this is something that has been highlighted in the research in this field (Corrius et al., 2016). This aspect can be mitigated by 'pre editing' the source text and by eliminating any ambiguous or binary use of language at source, which may serve as a way to reduce the number of opportunities for uncovering bias. A counterargument that could be offered here is about the effect of the queering process, which, rather than subverting, may prescriptively impose a new set of linguistic standards. This 'normalization' may be imposed or requested by the client's brief, which 'dictates' the style and language to be used in the translation products. Within this context, translators may be seen as operating as systemic perpetrators of alternative meanings, working within well-identified and identifiable constraints.

Catering for communities as diverse as the European, South American, and Middle Eastern ones is what posed the main challenge for students and put to the test their queering abilities. Some of the languages included in the project were found to require more effort when it came to locating adequate resources or parallel texts produced by organizations similar to the client's. For example, throughout the years the Arabic-speaking students reported that finding and using the type of terminology required by the client meant lengthy research and ultimately relying on the client's own Arabic-speaking contacts to tweak their final translations, which would be frowned upon in a real-life scenario, seeing as clients approach professional translators in the knowledge that they will know which resources to use. Despite redirecting students to official governmental and non-governmental resources available online, it was noted that the restrictions in place in Arabic-speaking countries in relation to matters regarding politics, sex, and religion (Nader, 2018) resulted in a much more limited variety of locally sourced sexual health resources compared to other languages and regions. This seems to align with scholarly analyses on translating into Arabic and the clash with the institutional obstacles at play when discussing the politics of translation in Arabic-speaking countries:

> One of the primary obstacles encountered while translating into Arabic is the connection of the Arabic language with religious authorities: this creates an occasional inability to be open to innovations in areas such as philosophy, human and life sciences. For instance, topics related to politics, sex and religion are prohibited from being dealt with in Arabic books and media; therefore, the majority of translators [refrain] from translating anything of that kind in order to avoid fines, accountability, or even imprisonment – in addition to escaping from any abuse of their religious or moral reputation in society (Al-Sammak 2015). A chaotic situation [ensues] for translation, caused by translating parts of a whole as well as by using poor sources. (Nader, 2018, p. 374)

It was mentioned in Section 5 that the purpose of queer pedagogy and translation is also to uncover ignorance or knowledge around ignorance (Shlasko, 2005). Although a post-survey chat was not run with the students, and therefore further clarification about particular comments could not be sought, a handful of comments seemed to confirm that an opening was created into the students' knowledge that something might need to be looked into differently and that new realities are possible. This could be interpreted as the realization of the ultimate aim of the pedagogy of discomfort, that is, self-reflection and a call to action. Another relevant point to be made as a direct response to the comments is that, in some students' view, it was not easy for them to talk about sexual health issues in relation to their own culture, and the fact that the project's audience would be mainly UK based made them feel more comfortable, as if they were in fact facilitating ideas or imposing cultural traits and practices perceived as 'other', with the tutor acting as the mediator in this 'identity transfer' process.

The tutor's role and their relationship with students indeed affected the mood and the general enjoyability of the translation tasks. What matters is that tutors are conscious that the learning environment is the aspect they (to some extent) can control or influence by organizing their teaching and shaping students' experiences (Marshall et al., 2014). The trust developed within this relationship, and the perception that the students have of the educator can affect the smooth running of the project and adherence to the client's brief. Tutors must plant the seeds of change in the classroom by encouraging students to critique inequality and sexism, since translators are major agents of change and meaning, and they must be conscious of the ethical, social, and ideological ramifications of their decisions. This should be accomplished by devising a methodology that enables students to work with a variety of texts incorporating a variety of challenges, so as to elicit a response from them and encourage them to take a position to actively and reflectively act upon those triggers, while at the same time directing them towards gender-positive and queer-positive productions of meaning. Additionally, this would raise their knowledge of their participation in the translation process and help them take responsibility for their interventions (De Marco & Toto, 2019).

The (queer) tutor's role must therefore be seen as an attempt at infiltrating the system to gently disrupt it from within, an educational 'Trojan horse' which mitigates the risks otherwise associated with a seemingly confrontational hetero-sexist environment. It is an attempt to 'decenter and destabilize the heterosexual normalization that so constructs the students we teach' (Pinar, 2009, p. 5). The core idea and suggestion is to facilitate a 'humanizing pedagogy' (Freire, 1993, p. 68), one that favours dialogue with students and allows them to co-create knowledge, whether contributing with their own existing experience or with newly formed units of learning, steeped in authenticity (in the teaching). It is a co-directed process which relies on the tutor being a facilitator, rather than the only centre of information (Cranton, 2016). This, however, should not be mistaken for a teacher-centric approach to learning: in fact, the onus is primarily shifted onto the students by providing them with a safe and open educational environment where they can freely explore their convictions, listen critically, and make their own informed decisions in relation to industry-led tasks. It is about emancipatory learning in which people critically examine their perceptions to be open to alternatives (Cranton, 2016).

This may be perceived as an agenda-pushing stance, but inclusion, self-assertiveness, compassion, and respect cannot be regarded as some sort of devious agenda. If the role of the educator is to disrupt students' knowledge in order to make way for new beginnings, new teachings, and new attitudes towards the world around them, then the core of these beliefs urgently needs revisiting. The correlation between queer theory and pedagogy stands on the shoulders of binary knowledge and the desire to overturn normalization (Luhmann, 1998). What the tutor is expected to do is disregard identities in the classroom and focus on the potential for translation success, for commercial viability, without however compromising each student's integrity. It is an ethical approach to teaching focused on transformative learning: it implies the promotion of values such as inclusiveness and the facilitation of new levels of awareness (Ettling, 2012). Because the task being discussed is part of a project management simulation and is attached to the publication of the students' work online, the margin for negotiation which would normally be expected to occur in a real-life workflow/situation is erased and replaced by quasi-market conditions where the students accept their role and their task in order to gain experience. This experiential element and the novelty effect of the task appear to overcome any learned resistance or bias towards the content at stake. In fact, the content itself was not found to be particularly triggering or displeasing, whereas the internal dynamics within each simulated agency and the translation workflows emerged as the main points of discussion in the surveys.

The collaborative nature of the task undertaken by the students and their dialogic relationship with the client somewhat preconfigures and confirms the essential 'extra-linguistic' nature of the translation profession, that is, its reliance on exchanges which go above and beyond the mere linguistic transfer of words and expressions. It is the product of extended collaboration (Baer, 2021). As such, the activity was characterized by its intrinsically voluntary nature, given the non-professional standing of the students involved, which can nevertheless be appreciated as a radical practice involving future translators providing a service otherwise denied by their own institutions (Baldo, 2021). Since the individual language solutions adopted in the translations were not assessed on this occasion, this could be an aspect for further investigation which could highlight different cognitive and social processes at play during the translation workflow. It may also uncover a series of further ethical issues not explored as part of the present case study.

In the previous sections, attention was paid to concepts surrounding current discourses on translation, queerness, and pedagogy. The case study analysed here has shown the effect and influence on students that queer pedagogy, when suitably contextualized and supported, can have on them and how it can help them question, query, and 'queer' their own beliefs in the light of extra-curricular endeavours which prepare them for the industry, in this case the translation industry. The transformative power of language in translation as a social vessel for change (De Marco & Toto, 2019) reveals 'the process through which gender is constructed, imposed and even naturalized through language [challenging] both the self-evidence of nature and the need to rely on the gender binary in order to speak, communicate, and be understood' (Gérardin-Laverge, 2020, p. 104).

Trust in the tutor's approach to the topic and their ability to handle discussions and situations in the classroom was also noticed as a catalyst for engagement, so much so that the centrality of the role of the tutor was mentioned several times in the accompanying module evaluation form distributed across the years. Although the translations as such were not assessed as part of the module assessment scheme but were instead revised for quality by more senior students and, at times, by the client themselves, there was indeed pressure on the part of the students to perform to a high standard, to a professional standard, so as not to let their tutor and their client down. As posited by Corrius and colleagues (2016, p. 71), 'we cannot exclude students' pressure when their tasks are evaluated and we might even wonder whether it is positive that students' response is affected by the lecturers' overt commitment to gender concerns'. This would also develop accountability for their interventions and increase their awareness of their role within the translation process (De Marco & Toto, 2019).

The teacher–student relationship, however, is not confined to the classroom only: students rely on the tutor for all sorts of matters, such as advice, guidance, and personal and academic problems. The tutor, in this particular context, shares their own experience of the translation industry and episodes of a personal nature that have moulded them into the practitioner they have become. The classroom is only one of the many scenarios and settings in which this relationship is played out; therefore, the dialogue between the two parties is ongoing and not limited to class times only.

As observed in the analysis of the responses to the survey, students rely on their tutor to make sense of new worlds and this trust relationship, which is a tenet of transformative and emancipatory learning, cannot and should not be abused. What is needed between translation trainers and translation students, where the goal of training is to raise awareness of positions of influence, is a more fruitful conversation about the power of translators in society, with its associated political and ideological consequences (Castro, 2013b): it is about the acknowledgement of power and privilege in this relationship to avoid as much as possible asymmetries in the dynamics (Page, 2016). Trust stems from personal power (charisma, expertise, loyalty) rather than position power (formal authority, control) (Cranton, 2016), and such power should be revered as a privilege rather than a distancing point which further increases and/or exacerbates hierarchical structures. It turns teaching into 'the creation of a new condition of knowledge, the creation of an original learning disposition' (Felman, 1987, p. 80). As such, translation is seen as not happening in a vacuum or as a sterile and static activity; translation trainees require a figure that speaks positively and in an encouraging way about certain topics, someone who is knowledgeable and someone who is not afraid of tackling sensitive issues in the classroom in order to multiply the possibilities for knowledge in queer pedagogy.

Translation therefore relies on small acts of queer disruption and multiple 'coming outs', in which the signifiers 'out' the translator's relationship with themselves and with the text through the inner workings being played out on the page. It is a relentless reformulation and chameleonic reimagining of the self and of the Other, ever-changing on the basis of the expectations of the target audience, the client, the labour market, the genre being translated, and so on. The multifaceted natured of this academic discipline is what also keeps it relevant and alive,[13] especially when it challenges heteronormative assumptions and creates new ways of understanding gender and sexuality across cultures. Through the act of translation, queer identities and experiences can be given visibility in contexts where they may otherwise be silenced or marginalized. Translation can also create new opportunities for cross-cultural dialogue and understanding, as it enables the exploration and negotiation of differences in language, culture, and identity. It is a game of chess being played around the choices made, the ensuing scrutiny, the afterthoughts, but also the pride in the choices made and the visibility acquired. By disrupting traditional power

---

[13] The name and consolidation of translation studies as an interdiscipline was the work of openly gay scholar and activist James S. Holmes (Larkosh, 2017). See also *The name and nature of translation studies*, first presented at the Third International Congress of Applied Linguistics (Copenhagen, 1972).

structures and promoting alternative ways of seeing and experiencing the world, (queer) translation and its teaching can contribute to broader social and political movements for gender and sexual justice, thus requiring a critical and reflexive approach to the translation process, and an awareness of the ways in which language and culture intersect with issues of gender and sexuality. It is a constantly evolving practice as queer identities and expressions continue to change and expand.

Appendix

Full extracts from the open questions in the anonymous surveys (grammatically edited)

Q2. Please explain how comfortable you were translating the text in terms of content (i.e. did you feel comfortable translating sexual-health-related materials)?

2019–20 Survey

- I was checking the work of another translator. I was comfortable as I approached it as one of my jobs.
- Overall, I found it quite easy to translate the text and the terms were similar in my language. Therefore, I would definitely be interested in working again with this subject.
- I was confident; however, I had to do some research as certain terms are different in my target language/had to explain or rephrase it.
- I was absolutely comfortable translating the content. I believe it is not something to be ashamed about; sexual health is an important issue that must be taken into consideration, and I was glad to be able to provide information about it to people who need it.
- Some terms I was not comfortable translating.
- I felt comfortable as I already knew a little bit about the subject.
- I was completely at ease with the content.
- I felt comfortable translating sexual-health-related materials, despite my unfamiliarity with the topic, as throughout the project I was able to educate not just others but also myself about it.
- I have always been very comfortable with sex-related topics, since I grew up with open-minded parents, with whom I have always discussed any doubts or questions I might have had on my sexual life. Moreover, I felt it was my duty to be fully informed, so I have been reading books and articles on the topic since I was very young.
- Yes.
- Yes I felt comfortable translating sexual-health-related materials.

2020–1 Survey

- Very comfortable.
- I felt confident as I am trying to educate myself; however, sometimes some words were new to me.
- I was comfortable enough to translate it but I only reviewed the text; it made me feel a little uneasy that people have to do this in order to have a sexual relationship with people.
- Yes.
- I was comfortable translating my part of translation.
- I did not have a lot of knowledge on the topic, but I took the project as an opportunity to develop it.
- It was a medical text and for raising social awareness so it was interesting.
- Yes, no difference to any other translation.
- I was confident in supporting the team during this task. I was aware of different cultures and different perceptions of sexual-health-related materials in order to be absolutely ready to help in case of any inconvenience due to possible uncomfortable situations.
- I felt confident translating sexual-health-related materials, although I had to educate myself to acquire further knowledge about the subject matter.
- Having done the glossary, I felt comfortable with the topic itself. Nevertheless, a few terms were very specific to the medical field and required a lot more time to find the pertinent TL equivalent, especially when not inserted in a context.
- Yes, I felt comfortable translating sexual-health-related texts.
- Although it is not very easy to talk about sexual health issues in my culture, this project audience was UK based, so I was quite comfortable with it.
- I was fully comfortable translating the text because it was educational.
- I did not have any concerns in terms of the topic of the text.
- The subject matter was quite new to me and I was anxious about translating it. However, as I started researching about the topic, it became interesting and motivating for I was gaining more knowledge about it. In the end, the translation became something that I enjoyed.

2021–2 Survey

- Yes, as it is a topic that should be part of everyone's knowledge and people should be more aware of it.
- I had never translated anything like this before, so I was afraid of making a mistake, because sexual diseases are still a field of medicine and it is a big responsibility to use good terminology.

- I felt comfortable translating sexual-health-related content. However, since I was not familiarised with the topic I felt I had to educate myself beforehand.
- I was comfortable, but it was also a challenge since I didn't have much knowledge of this field.
- Very comfortable, because it is a subject health prevention [topic].
- Yes, I was very comfortable with it since it was not an unfamiliar topic for me.
- Somewhat comfortable.
- I felt a little bit uncomfortable because I don't totally agree with the LGBTQ community. However, I wanted to challenge myself and prove that I can be professional and to expand my knowledge.
- The content did not affect my moral convictions.
- Yes. I was somehow confident. This is my first time being a mediator of sexual-health-related material.
- I was pretty confident given the fact that I already knew what the terms were and I already have a good knowledge about the topic.
- The equivalent terminology is easy to find.

Q4a. Please elaborate further on the previous answer, i.e. how much the course prepared you to translate sexual-health-related content in terms of inclusive language, terminology, register, etc.

2019–20 Survey

- I had no preparation regarding the terminology and the translation at word level; however, learning about ethics in translation allowed me to be more comfortable with the translation.
- Although it is not a topic we discuss on a daily basis, I feel like I was prepared to perform this task as my tutor gave me enough guidance to perform this and much more.
- They keep the course and the documents we have to translate quite general. This was the first time for me to translate a sexual-health-related text but I enjoyed it.
- The course has provided me with translation strategies to deal with the implementation of inclusive language, even in my target language. I have learned how to get to the right resources I would obtain my terminology from, and also how to identify when a formal/informal register is needed. I have been taught about ethics in translation, meeting the deadlines and making sure you provide a good-quality translation.
- The course prepared us well to be ready to translate sexual health content.

- The course has prepared me to translate sexual-health-related content as I have been taught how to use inclusive language, the way to speak about subjects.
- The course covers a number of topics that equip students with theoretical and practical knowledge, such as translation processes and procedures, pre-translation text analysis and terminology research just to name a few.
- The course I am attending pretty much covers all aspects and topics in translation but in regard to sexual-health-related content I believe that there has not been much time invested in these. But the lecturer has definitely been very present in guiding and providing us with feedback throughout the project whenever needed.
- We had never had a chance to translate something sexual health related before. However, the vocabulary was not an issue, as we managed to find everything using parallel texts and dictionaries. The real challenge was keeping the information easy to understand for a wide audience, with such a delicate topic, and keeping the language informal and gender neutral. During the translation course, especially thanks to the language-specific sessions, we were prepared to face and solve these problems professionally.
- Terminology and use of language.
- Well prepared.

2020–1 Survey

- The course prepared me very well.
- The course prepared me for the process of the translation and I felt very satisfied.
- I know there was software I could use and that I should never translate literally unless it's an option for semantic meaning.
- Last year we learned how to search for terms and make a glossary; this year we learned more about register and inclusive language.
- The course fully prepared me to translate sexual-health-related content.
- I was aware of inclusive language from previous seminars and I was equipped with the skills to target my research and approach the task.
- I need training so my knowledge becomes relevant to the modern world.
- All the above were provided. Some of which were explained in class.
- The course fully prepared me to engage with specific different areas. There were many medical terms although some of them related to sexual health terminology and therefore I felt confident to overcome any issue during the project using the skills learned in class.
- The course has provided me with knowledge of register and adaptation of the language in context. It trained me on how to best adhere to the clients'

requirements, to adapt the language according to the brief, function, intention and target audience and to make the most appropriate decisions.

- The course created the basis to question/explore the brief in order for the terminology to be better suited to a particular TL variant. Modules where gender in language is explored also created the basis for an awareness of how it can be unintentionally biased and how to try and avoid it.
- I had a presentation about the website we were translating as well as the client who gave us specific details about the project, a glossary with all the common words that would appear in the text.
- I did a community interpreting course in the past and have been working as an interpreter ever since, which is more or less similar to my current translation course; however, the amount of tools and experience that I have learnt since the start of the course is amazing and it helped me to work on this project.
- The course was the pillar to the elaboration of the project. The knowledge was the basis of the project.
- We widely discussed how important it is to identify the needs of the client and what type of target text is expected, what the audience would be and other important aspects. We also talked about the market so I already felt prepared in that aspect.
- This course gave me the necessary tools and knowledge for the translation activity. However, I was not prepared to carry out a translation on sexual-health-related content.

2021–2 Survey

- Everyone was aware of the inclusive language to be used and reference materials were provided.
- In order to do my work, I have gone to different websites, I have read up on textual diseases and I have consulted different parallel texts, so I feel much more comfortable and prepared. Although in translation there is always room for improvement and more research.
- To begin with, I firmly believe that we should work more on inclusive translation. Most languages we translate into are very different from English in terms of gender, which can make it difficult to produce inclusive translations. Regarding terminology, maybe we were not familiarised with sexual-health-related terms, but the course prepared us to be able to find reliable sources to consult the terms.
- Very well, I had enough material and also, I knew where to search.
- The tutor showed us techniques to use inclusive language.

- We discussed it in some of the previous subjects but not in an extensive way I would say. I feel like I have obtained a lot more knowledge about inclusive language from my own experience and research on the internet, but then again, it is something that interests me personally.
- Through the lectures on the translation process and procedures, I learnt how to deal with specific issues related to culture and other types including gender. However, I am still not very familiar with non-binary gender approaches in translation into my target language (French). I realized a real gap in my knowledge of how much things are evolving in that respect.
- We did not touch on inclusive language in depth. However, we were taught how to research and find reliable sources which could replace the lack of inclusive language training.
- The course prepared us to do qualitative research, and in my opinion, it is enough to be able to translate that kind of materials.
- The [module] leader has made everything easy for us as students; I was fully prepared and was fully aware of the content and how important it is to use an inclusive language, terminology and register. Especially the fact that the people in charge of the app came to see us in person to explain in depth about the app and were open to our point of view as students and answered any questions we had in mind.
- We did very few lessons on 'how to queer our language'.
- We already discussed how to find specific terms related to the content.

Q6. Describe and comment in full on your experience of working on this translation (for example, were there elements that were challenging, enjoyable, or tangibly different from other translation tasks?).

2019–20 Survey

- The challenge was to find equivalent terms in my native language; however, after further research I have solved any translation problems that have occurred.
- The challenging part was adapting the language so that all the speakers from different countries share a language they would understand.
- The syntax in my target language is different. I had to cut some of the repetitions like the word syphilis. I had to do some research for some terms. What I realised is that in my target language they talk about syphilis but not as explicitly and detailed and directly as for this project. I liked that I was able to 'speak' to the reader by implementing 'you'. Normally when I read any text about health they keep it formal rather than informal. It was

a challenge as I know that my work and other classmates' work will be published but at the same time I put more effort in my translation.

- Meeting the client and getting to know the project and the website have definitely been a plus. Knowing the effect it was going to have has motivated me to do an even better job. I have also enjoyed learning more about sexual health and prevention while doing my research. The most challenging part of the translation was probably the medical part and making sure every term was correct and widely used in my target country.
- I enjoyed translating the article but I reached a point where I couldn't find a correct translation for some terminology to use it in my target text. I looked in online dictionaries and some online articles. It was really hard.
- I really enjoyed this translation project as it was something that I have never translated before.
- I have thoroughly enjoyed the process and the brief. This was the first time I translated this particular subject and whilst I have an adequate knowledge on the subject, I still had to do some research. I have also learned a lot of new information on the way. I enjoyed elements of creativity of this task, specifically trying to manipulate the language in terms of gender and inclusive language. It made a very big difference meeting the client and receiving the brief directly from him.
- I am really happy I was given this project to work on alongside my colleagues. It surely took me out of my comfort zone in terms of working as a team but the overall experience has been constructive. Also, the purpose of this collaboration has inspired me personally: I realised more that the work of a translator is always valuable and also that from small to big translations the final product will somehow always have an impact on the reader.
- It was a very enjoyable experience, knowing that our contribution is going to make an actual difference in the life of many. As I mentioned above, I was comfortable with the topic. However, I found combining gender-neutral and informal language with such delicate information challenging. In fact, in my language (Italian) we use a more formal register in medical texts and we avoid repetitions. Therefore, lowering the register without affecting the readability of the text and the clarity of information was difficult at times.
- No.
- I found the task enjoyable; it gave me an opportunity to experience working in a team.

2020–1 Survey

- It was an enjoyable and very interesting translation to do.
- New terms that needed additional research were quite challenging; however, overall it was very enjoyable.
- I found the review of the translation hard as I was having to review in my foreign language and so I'm not too sure of the grammatical rules in the language so I was a little apprehensive to change anything other than some words that I knew could be written a little better for the overall flow and space constraints of the text.
- I enjoyed working for this translation since I think the cause is important.
- I enjoyed working on this project and appreciate the work dynamics monitoring by the PMs.
- It was an inspiring experience in terms of the importance of translators as activists. Language should be up to date with the society and the current variety of gender identities. In terms of the project as such, it was challenging but also rewarding to manage my role and perform the assigned tasks within deadlines. I have tried to be a valuable team player and to step in when other members were not as proactive. It was a good training for a real professional scenario.
- Hope to take more similar projects.
- As proofreader – time managing – other commitments were essential too; therefore time was an obstacle for me in this translation. However, I managed to finalise it on time.
- There were some difficulties in finding parallel texts for some of the languages we have provided but this is purely based on the feedback I have received by the members of my agency.
- It was enjoyable and constructive. It fulfilled me with insight on what happens behind a translation project, the various roles and expectations. How to ensure reliability and quality of product and quality of service.
- It is great to be part of a project that will have a significant social impact.
- As it was a health-related text, I had to ensure I had a high level of knowledge of the topic in order to ensure the information in the target language was correct, which was a challenge as there were a few terms which I was not familiar with, so in order to find equivalents in the TL I had to research the terms to fully understand.
- There were not many parallel texts online, other than UK based clinic called Mayo Clinic's website.
- The project was really challenging because I was not fully familiarized with the terms.

- The hardest part of the project was to fit it in my schedule and managing the project was a huge challenge but collaborating with everyone was great.
- This project was different from other translation tasks that I did. It was a medical text, therefore requiring some knowledge of medical terminologies. After some readings across the topic in my other language, it became clear and I benefitted from it as well.

2021–2 Survey

- Overall it was a really good experience as it represented real-life scenarios. It prepared me to see which problems I might encounter when working with other people. However, it did make me realise that probably working individually in a project such as this one would have been easier for stylistic and consistency reasons. It was really interesting and enhanced my interest in localisation.
- The tricky part has been with the terminology, because in my language there is no corpus, glossary or anything like that. It has not been easy because there is no corpus, no glossary or anything like that. However, in my country there is a lot of talk about sexual diseases, so I have been able to consult different websites, such as the one of the government of my country, which talk openly about the subject. The problem is that the terminology varies a lot from one site to another and I have had to make decisions about it. However, the good part is that I have learned a lot about this issue. Actually, the best thing about being a translator is that you never stop learning new things because in order to translate you have to document, read, learn and understand. Therefore, in addition to giving me work experience, this assignment has been very satisfying in terms of learning.
- Personally, it was quite an enjoyable experience because I am really interested in gender-inclusive translation and this was a great opportunity to practise my previously acquired skills.
- Challenging and enjoyable to learn a new field and expand on my knowledge.
- It was a great immersion in a real-life scenario, I felt happy to be part of such a project due to its nature; I also experienced the challenges of it such as communication problems with managers but it was all positive.
- It was very positive; the project was very interesting and important. I think it is vital to normalise the discussion about STIs and sexual health in general since it still seems to be taboo in some environments. I am also happy since I've never had an opportunity to translate materials around this topic, so for me it was an invaluable experience. I put a lot of effort into creating a translation written in an inclusive language and this was the part that was

challenging at times. Unfortunately, I feel like this was not of such importance to other members of the agency, e.g. several of the fragments have been
changed by the proofreader into a non-inclusive one.

- My overall experience was insightful, as it helped me discover how delicate it
is to deal with gender bias in texts to be translated and how important it is to
pay attention to certain details to fulfil the brief for such a specific project. It
was challenging to maintain consistency throughout because nature always
interfered, but self-revision helped. I had to pay extra attention to specialist
terminology to make sure there was no mix-up. I enjoyed learning new
realities awaiting me in the industry that is becoming more diverse and
inclusive.

- I enjoyed the overall experience. However, the role of proofreading I didn't
enjoy too much as we didn't have too much of practice and I needed some
more context when proofreading. The challenging part was to accept that not
everyone would take the project very seriously and that even if I put in a lot of
effort, people would not do the same. In terms of material and content, all was
clear and the client provided us with visual support which helped a lot. Maybe
the process of getting something to translate should be more specific and the
tutor should make a chart so people could visually see the process and steps to
follow when implicated in a project like this. For example, to have a mind
map of the steps: 1st terminologist, 2nd send back to PM, 3rd PM to send
material to translators, 4th send back to PM, etc. As a lot of people used to not
respect the steps and tried to rush and because of that, issues appeared and the
level of anxiety was very high.

- It was a great experience in terms of communication and cooperation as
a team to complete the project. The focus was more on the quality and
organisational process.

- At the beginning, I was so nervous about starting with the project as I was so
looking forward to producing impeccable work for my first experience. True
it was challenging to work with other people with different personalities;
however, it was also good to reflect on my self-experience on how I would
react in the real workplace. I have learnt that working with others comes as
a package where there is certainly a positive and a negative side of it; if it is
well handled, working as a team is just amazing. This experience was surely
different from other experiences I had in the past as it brought the feel of the
real word into it!

- I did enjoy the topic because it's a topic I like and I already know about;
I found it challenging working with people that had close to zero knowledge
about that, saying and writing very wrong and not very inclusive things.

References

Alhazmi, A. A. & Kaufmann, A. (2022). Phenomenological qualitative methods applied to the analysis of cross-cultural experience in novel educational social contexts. *Frontiers in Psychology*, 13, article 785134, pp. 1–12. http://doi.org/10.3389/fpsyg.2022.785134.

Association of Translation Companies (ATC) (2019). *Code of professional conduct.* Available at: https://atc.org.uk/wp-content/uploads/2018/06/ATC-Code-of-Professional-Conduct.pdf.

Association of Translation Companies (ATC) (2022). *A quick guide to language support.* Available at: https://atc.org.uk/wp-content/uploads/A-Quick-Guide-to-Language-Support-2022.pdf.

Baer, B. J. (2021). *Queer theory and translation studies: Language, politics, desire.* London: Routledge. https://doi.org/10.4324/9781315514734.

Baker, M. (1996). Corpus-based translation studies: The challenges that lie ahead. In H. Somers, ed., *Terminology, LSP and translation: Studies in language engineering in honor of Juan C. Sager.* Amsterdam: John Benjamins, pp. 175–86.

Baker, M. (2010). Translation and activism: Emerging patterns of narrative community. *Massachusetts Review*, 47(3), pp. 462–84.

Baldo, M. (2021). Queer feminisms and the translation of sexual health. In Ş. Susam-Saraeva & E. Spišiaková, eds., *The Routledge handbook of translation and health*, 1st ed. London: Routledge, pp. 314–30. https://doi.org/10.4324/9781003167983.

Barker, M. J. & Scheele, J. (2016). *Queer: A graphic history.* London: Icon Books.

Bassnett, S. (2011). The translator as cross-cultural mediator. In K. Malmkjaer & K. Windle, eds., *The Oxford handbook of translation studies.* Oxford: Oxford University Press, pp. 77–85. https://doi.org/10.1093/oxfordhb/9780199239306.013.0008.

Bodrov-Krukowski, I. (2020). Internationalization vs. localization (i18n vs l10n): What's the difference? Available at: https://lokalise.com/blog/internationalization-vs-localization/.

Boler, M. (1999). A pedagogy of discomfort: Witnessing and the politics of anger and fear. In M. Boler, ed., *Feeling power: Emotions and education.* New York: Routledge, pp. 175–202.

Britzman, D. P. (1995). Is there a queer pedagogy? Or, stop reading straight. *Educational Theory*, 45(2), pp. 151–65. https://doi.org/10.1111/j.1741-5446.1995.00151.x.

Bryson, M. & De Castell, S. (1993). Queer pedagogy: Praxis makes im/perfect. *Canadian Journal of Education/Revue Canadienne de l'éducation*, 18(3), pp. 285–305. https://doi.org/10.2307/1495388.

Carcelén-Estrada, A. (2018). Translation and activism. In F. Fernández & J. Evans, eds., *Routledge handbook of translation and politics*. New York: Routledge, pp. 254–69.

Carlson, R. & Corliss, J. (2011). Imagined commodities: Video game localization and mythologies of cultural difference. *Games and Culture*, 6(1), pp. 61–82.

Castro, O. (2013a). Introduction: Gender, language and translation at the crossroads of disciplines. *Gender and Language*, 7(1), pp. 5–12. https://doi.org/10.1558/genl.v7i1.5.

Castro, O. (2013b). Talking at cross-purposes? The missing link between feminist linguistics and translation studies. *Gender and Language*, 7(1), pp. 35–58. https://doi.org/10.1558/genl.v7i1.35.

Chartered Institute of Linguists (CIOL) (2017). *Code of professional conduct*. Available at: www.ciol.org.uk/sites/default/files/Code_5.pdf.

Corrius, M., De Marco, M. & Espasa, E. (2016). Situated learning and situated knowledge: Gender, translating audiovisual adverts and professional responsibility. *The Interpreter and Translator Trainer*, 10(1), pp. 59–75. http://dx.doi.org/10.1080/1750399X.2016.1154343.

Cranton, P. (2016). *Understanding and promoting transformative learning: A guide to theory and practice*, 3rd ed. Sterling, VA: Stylus Publishing.

De Marco, M. & Toto, P. (2019). The future of academia, gender and queer pedagogy: Concluding remarks. In M. De Marco & P. Toto, eds., *Gender approaches in the translation classroom: Training the doers*. London: Palgrave Macmillan, pp. 189–93.

Dunlosky, J., Rawson, K. A., Marsh, E. J., Nathan, M. J. & Willingham, D. T. (2013). Improving students' learning with effective learning techniques: Promising directions from cognitive and educational psychology. *Psychological Science in the Public Interest*, 14(1), pp. 4–58. https://doi.org/10.1177/1529100612453266.

Durban, C. & Melby, A. (2008). *Translation: Buying a non-commodity*. Available at: https://atanet.org/wp-content/uploads/2020/06/translation_buying_guide.pdf.

Elder, G. S. (1999). Queerying boundaries in the geography classroom. *Journal of Geography in Higher Education*, 23(1), pp. 86–93.

Ettling, D. (2012). Educator as change agent. In E. W. Taylor & P. Cranton, eds., *The handbook of transformative learning: Theory, research, and practice*. San Francisco, CA: John Wiley & Sons, pp. 536–51.

Felman, S. (1987). *Jacques Lacan and the adventure of insight: Psychoanalysis in contemporary culture*. Boston, MA: Harvard University Press.

Fishman, J. (1991). *Reversing language shift: Theoretical and empirical foundations of assistance to threatened languages*. Clevedon: Multilingual Matters.

Floros, G. (2020). Pedagogical translation in school curriculum design. In M. Ji & S. Laviosa, eds., *The Oxford handbook of translation and social practices*. Oxford: Oxford University Press, pp. 279–99. https://doi.org/10.1093/oxfordhb/9780190067205.001.0001.

Foucault, M. (1972). *The archaeology of knowledge and the discourse on language*. New York: Dorset Press.

Freire, P. (1993). *Pedagogy of the oppressed*. New York: Continuum.

Gérardin-Laverge, M. (2020). Queering language, de-naturalizing gender. Translated by L. Garnier. In *Cahiers du Genre*, 69(2), pp. 31–58. Available at: www.cairn-int.info/journal-cahiers-du-genre-2020-2-page-31.htm?WT.tsrc=pdf.

Ghazala, H. S. (2002). The translator's dilemma with bias. *Babel*, 48, pp. 147–62.

Giroux, H. (2013). A critical interview with Henry Giroux. *Global Education Magazine*, 1. Available at: www.globaleducationmagazine.com/critical-interview-henry-giroux/.

GTE Localize (2022). How to prepare an effective localization kit in 2022. Available at: https://gtelocalize.com/prepare-an-effective-localization-kit/.

Hatim, B. & Mason, I. (1997). *The translator as communicator*. London: Routledge.

Institute of Translation and Interpreting (ITI) (2013). *ITI code of professional conduct*. Available at: www.iti.org.uk/resource/iti-code-of-professional-conduct.html.

Ji, M. (2020). Translation and social practices. In M. Ji & S. Laviosa, eds., *The Oxford handbook of translation and social practices*. Oxford: Oxford University Press, pp. 1–21. http://dx.doi.org/10.1093/oxfordhb/9780190067205.013.2.

Ji, M., Sørensen, K. & Bouillon, P. (2020). User-oriented healthcare translation and communication. In M. Ji & S. Laviosa, eds., *The Oxford handbook of translation and social practices*. Oxford: Oxford University Press, pp. 430–51. https://doi.org/10.1093/oxfordhb/9780190067205.013.33.

Jiménez-Crespo, M. A. (2009). Conventions in localisation: A corpus study of original vs. translated web texts. *JoSTrans: The Journal of Specialised Translation*, 12, pp. 79–102. Available at: https://jostrans.org/issue12/art_jimenez.php.

Kedem, N. (2019). What is queer translation? *symplokē*, 27(1), pp. 157–83. www
.muse.jhu.edu/article/734656.

Kincheloe, J. (2008). *Critical pedagogy*. New York: Peter Lang.

Kopelson, K. (2002). Dis/integrating the gay/queer binary: Reconstructed
identity politics for a performative pedagogy. *College English*, 65(1),
pp. 17–35.

Larkosh, C. E. (2017). James S. Holmes, translation studies and the queer
ethics of the first person. In J. Santaemilia, ed., *Traducir para la igualdad
sexual = Translating for sexual equality*. Granada: Editorial Comares, pp.
137–72.

Laviosa, S. (2014a). *Translation and language education: Pedagogic
approaches explored*. London: Routledge.

Laviosa, S. (ed.). (2014b). Translation in the language classroom: Theory,
research and practice. Special issue of *The Interpreter and Translator
Trainer*, 8(1), pp. 1–7.

Lee, T. K. (2022). *Translation as experimentalism: Exploring play in poetics*.
Cambridge: Cambridge University Press. https://doi.org/10.1017/9781108
917292.

Luhmann, S. (1998). Queering/querying pedagogy? Or, pedagogy is a pretty
queer thing. In W. Pinar, ed., *Queer theory in education*. Mahwah, NJ:
Lawrence Erlbaum Associates, pp. 120–32.

Malmkjær, K. (2022). Introduction. In K. Malmkjær, ed., *The Cambridge
handbook of translation*. Cambridge: Cambridge University Press, pp.
1–10. https://doi.org/10.1017/9781108616119.001.

Markey, K., Graham, M. M., Tuohy, D. et al. (2023) Navigating learning
and teaching in expanding culturally diverse higher education settings.
Higher Education Pedagogies, 8(1). https://doi.org/10.1080/23752696.2023
.2165527.

Marshall, S., Fry, H. & Ketteridge, S. (2014). *A handbook for teaching and
learning in higher education: Enhancing academic practice*, 4th ed. London:
Routledge.

Matis, N. (2017). How to deal with questions during a translation project. *The
Chronicle*. Available at: www.ata-chronicle.online/featured/how-to-deal-
with-questions-during-a-translation-project/.

McLaren, P. (2003). Critical pedagogy: A look at the major concepts. In
A. Darder, M. Baltodano & R. D. Torres, eds., *The critical pedagogy reader*.
New York: Routledge Falmer, pp. 69–96.

Microsoft (2016). Localization of the user interface. Available at: https://learn
.microsoft.com/en-us/previous-versions/office/developer/sharepoint-2010/
ff955227(v=office.14).

Mitchell-Schuitevoerder, R. (2020). *A project-based approach to translation technology*. London: Routledge.

Munday, J. (2007). Translation and ideology. *The Translator*, 13(2), pp. 195–217. https://doi.org/10.1080/13556509.2007.10799238.

Munday, J. (2014). Text analysis and translation. In S. Bermann & C. Porter, eds., *A companion to translation studies*, 1st ed. Chichester: Wiley Blackwell, pp. 67–81.

Murray, H. & Smith, P. (eds.) (2013). *Closing the loop: Are universities doing enough to act on student feedback from course evaluation surveys?* London: Electric Paper.

Nader, M. (2018). Politics of translation in Arabic-speaking countries. In F. Fernández & J. Evans, eds., *The Routledge handbook of translation and politics*, 1st ed. London: Routledge, pp. 371–85. https://doi.org/10.4324/9781315621289.

Nord, C. (2022). Action/skopos theory. In F. Zanettin & C. Rundle, eds., *The Routledge handbook of translation and methodology*, 1st ed. London: Routledge, pp. 11–25. https://doi.org/10.4324/9781315158945.

O'Driscoll, S. (1996). Outlaw readings: Beyond queer theory. *Signs*, 22(1), pp. 30–51. Available at: http://www.jstor.org/stable/3175040?origin=JSTOR-pdf.

Page, M. L. (2016). LGBTQ inclusion as an outcome of critical pedagogy. *International Journal of Critical Pedagogy*, 7(1), pp. 115–42.

Pinar, W. F. (2009). Introduction. In W. Pinar, ed., *Queer theory in education*. Mahwah, NJ: Lawrence Erlbaum Associates, pp. 1–39.

Public Health England (2019). *Sexually transmitted infections and chlamydia screening in England: 2019*. Available at: https://assets.publishing.service.gov.uk/government/uploads/system/uploads/attachment_data/file/914249/STI_NCSP_report_2019.pdf.

Pym, A. (2011). Website localizations. In K. Malmkjaer & K. Windle, eds., *The Oxford handbook of translation studies*. Oxford: Oxford University Press, pp. 274–83. https://doi.org/10.1093/oxfordhb/9780199239306.013.0028.

Pym, A., Malmkjær, K., Gutiérrez-Colón Plana, M., Lombardero, A., & Soliman, F. (2013). *Translation and language learning: The role of translation in the teaching of languages in the European Union, a study*. Luxembourg: European Commission.

Quilty, A. (2017). *Queer provocations!* Exploring queerly informed disruptive pedagogies within feminist community-higher-education landscapes. *Irish Educational Studies*, 36(1), pp. 107–23. https://doi.org/10.1080/03323315.2017.1289704.

Richman Davidow, S. (2018). Queering sexual health: The intersection of sexual health and LGBTQ identities in Worcester, MA. *International*

Development, Community and Environment (IDCE), 220. Available at https://commons.clarku.edu/idce_masters_papers/220.

Robinson, D. (2003). *Performative linguistics: Speaking and translating as doing things with words*. London: Routledge.

RWS Trados (n.d.). What is a CAT tool? Translation 101. Available at: www .trados.com/solutions/cat-tools/translation-101-what-is-a-cat-tool.html.

Sauntson, H. (2008) The contributions of queer theory to gender and language research. In K. Harrington, L. Litosseliti, H. Sauntson, & J. Sunderland, eds., *Gender and language research methodologies*. Basingstoke: Palgrave Macmillan, pp. 271–82.

Shih, C. (2010). Ideological interference in translation: Strategies of translating cultural references. *Translation Journal*, 14(3). Available at: http://transla tionjournal.net/journal/53culture.htm.

Shlasko, G. D. (2005). Queer (v.) pedagogy. *Equity & Excellence in Education*, 38(2), pp.123–34. https://doi.org/10.1080/10665680590935098.

Spivak, G. (1992/2012). The politics of translation. In L. Venuti, *The translation studies reader*, 3rd ed. London: Routledge, pp. 312–30.

Spurlin, W. (2014a). Queering translation. In S. Bermann & C. Porter, eds., *A companion to translation studies*. Oxford: Blackwell, pp. 298–309.

Spurlin, W. (2014b). The gender and queer politics of translation: New approaches. *Comparative Literature Studies*, 51(2), pp. 201–14.

Spurlin, W. (2019). Queer theory and biomedical practice: The biomedicalization of sexuality/the cultural politics of biomedicine. *The Journal of Medical Humanities*, 40(1), pp. 7–20. https://doi.org/10.1007/s10912-018-9526-0.

Team Prepster (2022) What is PrEP? Available at: https://prepster.info/faq/ #FAQ01.

The Love Tank (2021). Long time no syphilis. Available at: www.longtimeno syph.info/.

The Love Tank (2021). PrEPster. Available at: https://prepster.info/.

The Preptrack Foundation (2020-2). Available at: https://preptrack.co.uk/.

The Well Project (2021). Why language matters: Facing HIV stigma in our own words. Available at: www.thewellproject.org/hiv-information/whylanguage-matters-facing-hiv-stigma-our-own-words.

Thomas-Reid, M. (2018). Queer pedagogy. *Oxford research encyclopedia of education*. Available at: https://oxfordre.com/education/display/10.1093/ acrefore/9780190264093.001.0001/acrefore-9780190264093-e-405.

Toro, E. (2014). How to localize rich media for your global market. *MultiLingual. Industry Focus: Better World. Core Focus: Localization*, October/November 2014, pp. 41–3.

Tymoczko, M. (2003). Ideology and the position of the translator: In what sense is a translator 'in between'?' In M. Calzada Pérez, ed., *Apropos of ideology: Translation studies on ideology – ideologies in translation studies.* Manchester: St. Jerome, pp. 181–201.

Venuti, L. (2017). *The translator's invisibility: A history of translation*, 1st ed. London: Routledge.

Warner, M. (1993). *Fear of a queer planet: Queer politics and social theory.* Minneapolis, MN: University of Minnesota Press.

Williams, J. & Chesterman, A. (2002). *The map: A beginner's guide to doing research in translation studies*. Manchester: St. Jerome.

World Health Organization (WHO) (2006). *Defining sexual health: Report of a technical consultation on sexual health, 28–31 January 2002.* Geneva: World Health Organization.

Xie, S. (2018). Translation and globalization. In J. Evans & F. Fernandez, eds., *The Routledge handbook of translation and politics*, 1st ed. London: Routledge, pp. 79–94. https://doi.org/10.4324/9781315621289.

Zanettin, F. & Rundle, C. (eds.) (2022). *The Routledge handbook of translation and methodology*, 1st ed. London: Routledge. https://doi.org/10.4324/9781315158945.

Acknowledgements

I am grateful to the *Language, Gender and Sexuality* series' editors, Helen Sauntson and Holly Cashman, for their interest in my work and for their continued support.

To Will Nutland: thank you for the premium work that you and your PrEPster team do for sexual health services in the UK, including advocating for PrEP in the UK; I am grateful for your belief in the power of translation as a force for good but, most of all, thank you for your friendship.

This Element would not have been possible without the effort and enthusiasm of my students, who believed in the projects they were assigned and understood how essential their role would be in the current climate of sexual terrorism. I could have acknowledged their effort as a group – instead, I strongly believe that each one of them should be acknowledged for their contribution and credited for their effort:

Adriana A., Adrianna R, Agata Hanna K., Agnieszka S., Agnieszka W., Aisha A., Aleksandra P., Alessia G., Alice S., Alison R. B., Americo B., Aminata D., Ana Rita S. M., Ana-Maria G., Andrei L., Angela D., Anna B., Anna C., Antonella B., Arianna K., Arianne M. L., Assia K., Ayse M., Bassma S., Bouchra L., Clarisse T., Cristina G., Daniela J., David B. D. C., Deisy Andreina O. T., Dominika M., Dora A., Elia D. S. R., Emilie J., Ewa J.-D., Filipa M. S., Francesca A., Francesco G., Georgia F., Giulia B., Hanane K., Harrison L., Iga K., Ilenia V., Ioana B., Irene P. M., Iwona B., Jagoda Z., Julia W., Justyna S., Karolina R., Keerthana Y., Khadra H., Khuzama M., Klaudiusz P., Liliya H., Lindalva B., Liudmila T., Lucia Manuela L. A., Makadidia O., Manar A. E. Z., Manuela C., Matthew P., Medhy M.-K.-N., Natalia F., Natalia K., Nicoleta S., Nirvana S., Oliwia P., Oumnia E. A., Paula M. M., Paula P. N., Paulina S., Raquel R. B., Reka H.-P., Reyes N., Roberto F., Rosanna G., Samia S., Sara V., Sarah E., Sarah F., Selena E., Sevil A., Silvia P., Silvia S., Simona M., Sonia C., Souhila L., Tai M., Umar B., Vadim C., Veronika K.-U., Waleed Z., Wiktoria T., Yonesse M., Zoila P. I.; Nadia Rahab (MA Translation course leader) and Zoubida Mostefai-Hampshire (BA Translation course leader).

Thank you also to Samuel Bell (Preptrack) for entrusting us with his magic app.

A special thank you to Marcella De Marco and Sergio Rigoletto for their friendship and precious input on various aspects of the survey structure and content.

Cambridge Elements ≡

Language, Gender and Sexuality

About the Series
Cambridge Elements in Language, Gender and Sexuality highlights the role of language in understanding issues, identities and relationships in relation to multiple genders and sexualities. The series provides a comprehensive home for key topics in the field which readers can consult for up-to-date coverage and the latest developments.

Language, Gender and Sexuality

Printed in the United States
by Baker & Taylor Publisher Services